Weakest Link
Quiz Book

Weakest Link
Quiz Book

**Over 1800 questions from
TV's toughest quiz show**

CARLTON
BOOKS

THIS IS A CARLTON BOOK

This edition published by Carlton Publishing Group 2001

20 Mortimer Street

London

WIT 3JW

A CIP catalogue for this book is available from the Library of Congress.

ISBN 1 84222 595 2

Design: Vicky Holmes
Editorial: David Ballheimer, Sarah Larter
Additional research: Jonathan Gibbs
Production: Garry Lewis

Contents

How To Play Weakest Link

So here's your chance to play *Weakest Link* at home. Have you got the knowledge, skill and nerve to take on the challenge and win? Or is your knowledge best suited to watching the show on television?

The aim of *Weakest Link* is to become the strongest link and finish the game with all the points that have been earned. With each round the aim is to reach the 125,000-point target. The quickest way to do this is to answer eight questions correctly. This means you have to rely on the ability of your fellow players as an incorrect answer could lose you any points accumulated in that round. The alternative is to "bank" the points when it comes to your turn, which means you keep the points so far but go back to the bottom of the chain. At the end of each round, the players eliminate the weakest link in the team until there are just two players left fighting for the points.

To succeed to the end of the game, you need to be ruthless, and know when work with your team-mates and when to dump them. Should you bank the points or risk losing them by answering your question? Have you got the confidence to get right to the top of the chain? Can you dispatch the dead wood and eject the idiot? Are you ready to play *Weakest Link*? Well here's how.

BEFORE PLAY STARTS:

Weakest Link is best played with four or more players.

- Every player needs paper and a pen or pencil. If you are playing against the clock you will also need a stopwatch.

- One person is designated the question-master for the game. You must then decide on an order of play. You could draw lots to see who goes first, or order the players alphabetically. With the start of each new round the first question is asked to the next person in the order.

- The ground rules for each game should be agreed before it begins. Options for organizing the game are:

Complete round: A round could consist of twenty questions, asked alternately to each player; each set of questions is arranged thus in the book.

Time Limit: You could decide to increase the pressure and play against the clock, as in the television show. The first round could be 2 minutes and 30 seconds long, with each subsequent round 10 seconds shorter until a seventh of 1 minute and 30 seconds. The question-master could keep time in the first round, with one of the eliminated players taking over for subsequent rounds. If you time your rounds, then you may well need to use more than one set of questions for each round.

If a chain is completed and eight questions are answered correctly then the points are banked and a new round begins.

- In every case the answer required—unless specified to the contrary— is the common usage name. For example, the answer to the question, "What name of the venomous hooded snake of India?" is cobra, not *naja naja*. Full names should be given—except where specified. This is because more than one possible answer could be acceptable; for instance, "Who became President of the US immediately after the assassination of Abraham Lincoln?", would need "President Andrew Johnson" as the answer, not simply "President Johnson", because there was another president with the same surname, Lyndon (Baines) Johnson. Where variations or alternatives to answers are acceptable, they are in brackets.

THE GAME

- Once the ground rules have been agreed among the players, the *Weakest Link* TV show can be imitated almost exactly. Each player is asked a question in turn, based on the agreed order of play. At the end of each round of questions, all the players write down their weakest link and, after 10 seconds, they must all stop and show who they have chosen. The person who most players have voted for is ejected from the game with those infamous words *"You are the Weakest Link. Goodbye."*

  In the event of a tie-break, those previously eliminated (or the question-master if it is the first round) can decide who should become the next weakest link.

Once each round is completed the game continues until there are just two players left. The players can either play one more round to accumulate points or go directly to the head-to-head (see below).

SCORING

The question-master keeps track of the score using the chains that are printed on the right-hand side of each set of questons. The first question at the bottom of a chain is worth 1,000 points, with each correctly answered question worth more points as you move up the chain. For each question that is answered correctly, the question-master moves up one place on the chain. If a question is answered incorrectly, all points in that chain are lost and the round starts again at the bottom.

If a player shouts "bank" when it comes to their turn, the score so far is written in one of the blank spaces underneath the chain. These points are banked and cannot be lost, however the chain must now start again with the banking player's next question.

At the end of each round the question-master writes the number of points that have been accumulated in the space provided at the top of the chain on the next page or on a separate piece of paper. The next round begins at the bottom of the chain on the 1,000-point question.

It is up to each player to decide whether to risk getting a question wrong and going back to the bottom of the chain or to bank the points gained so far and break the chain.

HEAD-TO-HEAD

The head-to-head consists of ten questions, five for each player. The question-master can decide who goes first, based on who has been the strongest link in previous rounds, or the players can flip a coin.

The winner of the head-to-head is the person who has the most correct answers after five questions have been asked to each contestant. In the event of a tie, the question-master moves on to the next set of head-to-head questions, and the game becomes a case of sudden death, the first person to answer incorrectly is eliminated, and the remaining player takes all the points for that game and is the strongest link.

PLAYING WITH LESS THAN FOUR PLAYERS

You will have to play *Weakest Link* slightly differently with any less than four players.

If there are three of you, you can play as if there were four or more players, although after one round two remaining players will go straight to the head-to-head. Alternatively, each player can be asked either a set of twenty questions by one of the other players or as many questions as possible within an agreed time limit. The player answering can choose to bank their points with each correct answer to build up their score or risk going back to the bottom of the chain if they answer incorrectly. The strongest link is the player with the most points accumulated after each has completed a round. This can also be played with two contestants.

And if you just want to practice playing the *Weakest Link*, you can test your own general knowledge by quizzing yourself.

Now, if you're ready, it's time to play Weakest Link.

Round One

1 In television, what was the nickname of the character played by Scott Baio on the sitcom *Happy Days*?

2 According to legend which saint drove the snakes of Ireland into the sea?

3 The Jim Henson-created mascot "Bad Andy" was recently dropped from the TV ads for which pizza chain?

4 U.S. Presidential elections take place on the first Tuesday after the first Monday of which month?

5 Who was the first woman to fly an airplane solo across the Atlantic Ocean?

6 What is the name of the oldest university in the United States?

7 In music, which Canadian singer wrote the songs "Woodstock" and "Big Yellow Taxi"?

8 In history, who was convicted for the assassination of Robert F. Kennedy?

9 How many rings are featured on the official Olympic flag?

10 In movies, Kevin Spacey won the 1999 Academy Award for Best Actor for his role in which film?

11 In industry, which country produces more of the world's wine: France or the United States?

12 In theatre, which British composer scored both *Jesus Christ Superstar* and *Cats*?

13 In sports, which former Cincinnati Reds manager was banned from baseball for gambling?

14 In morse code, how many dots does it take to send the letter "S"?

15 Born in 1895, which U.S. architect developed the 4-D house and popularized the Geodesic dome?

16. Which is the state bird of Florida: the mockingbird or the flamingo?

17. In 1848 six New York newspapers agreed to pool together forming what worldwide news service?

18. Which inventor was known as the "Wizard of Menlo Park?"

19. In mythology, which Greek warrior was slain by Paris after being wounded in his vulnerable heel?

20. Puerto Rican pop sensation, Enrique Jose Martin Morales IV performs under what name?

PREVIOUS TOTAL

125,000
75,000
50,000
25,000
10,000
5,000
2,500
1,000

BANKED

TOTAL

Answers

1	Chachi.	12	(Sir) Andrew Lloyd Webber.
2	St. Patrick.	13	Pete Rose.
3	Domino's Pizza.	14	Three.
4	November.	15	(Richard) Buckminster Fuller.
5	Amelia Earhart.		
6	Harvard University.	16	Mockingbird.
7	Joni Mitchell.	17	Associated Press.
8	Sirhan Sirhan.		
9	Five.	18	Thomas (Alva) Edison.
10	*American Beauty*.	19	Achilles.
11	France.	20	Ricky Martin.

Round Two

1 On television, which brand of cognac does *Saturday Night Live*'s "The Ladies Man" always have on hand?

2 Which media mogul married designer Diane Von Furstenburg in 2001?

3 In the Dr. Seuss story, *Horton Hears a Who*, what kind of animal is Horton?

4 In language, which three-word Latin phrase translates to "I came, I saw, I conquered?"

5 Pregnant, hanging and swinging are terms describing which portion of a ballot that has not been completely removed?

6 Which pacifist received the Nobel Peace Prize for helping to end China's domination of Tibet?

7 Which eccentric comedian did Jim Carrey portray in the movie *Man on the Moon*?

8 Which of these famous philosophers was Dutch: Kant or Spinoza?

9 In geography, which is the world's tallest waterfall?

10 What was the maiden name of the late Diana, Princess Of Wales?

11 In art, what "S" is the movement most associated with painter Salvador Dali?

12 In chemistry, which element from the Periodic Table combines with oxygen to form water?

13 In computer terms, what does the acronym DOS stand for?

14 Which short-lived dance craze inspired the 1990 movie *The Forbidden Dance*?

15 In economics, which animal represents a declining stock market?

16 In fashion, what "F" is a red, brimless hat named after a city in Morocco?

17 In television, what is the name of Homer's youngest daughter on *The Simpsons*?

18 In transport, "Y–Y–Z" are the code letters for which Canadian city's airport?

19 In astrology, which sign of the of the Zodiac is also called the water bearer?

20 In history, which state became the first to ratify the U.S. Constitution?

Answers	
1 Courvoisier.	14 The lambada.
2 Barry Diller.	15 Bear.
3 Elephant.	16 Fez.
4 Veni, Vedi, Vici.	17 Maggie.
5 Chad(s).	18 Toronto.
6 Dalai Lama.	19 Aquarius.
7 Andy Kaufman.	20 Delaware.
8 Spinoza.	
9 Angel Falls.	
10 Spencer.	
11 Surrealism.	
12 Hydrogen.	
13 Disc Operating System.	

Round Three

1   Led by Joe Namath, which was the the first AFL (American Football League) team to win pro football's Super Bowl?

2   Kofi Annan is currently the Secretary-General of which international organization?

3   What "A" is the automaker that manufactures the T.T. Roadster?

4   Located in Nottinghamshire, England, which wooded area was home to Robin Hood and his Merry Men?

5   In music, what is the stage name of "Bat Out Of Hell" singer Marvin Lee Aday?

6   Which American teacher was chosen to be the first private citizen in space?

7   In math, what is the square root of 121?

8   Often seen on warning signs, what two words are combined to form the term "HAZMAT"?

9   In science, what "W" is a Unit of Power equal to one joule per second?

10 Which company originally released the party game Twister in 1966?

11 Which *Playgirl* cover model gained renown as O.J. Simpson's houseguest?

12 If you are having kippers for breakfast, are you eating fish or berries?

13 In literature, which French physician wrote the book of rhyming prophesies titled "Centuries"?

14 According to the title of the Rob Schneider film, what is the profession of Deuce Bigelow?

15 In advertising, which snack food company's slogan describes its cookies as "uncommonly good?"

16 In jewelry, how many karats is pure gold?

17 Which magazine was founded by John F. Kennedy Jr in 1995?

18 "Semper fidelis," meaning "always faithful," is the motto of which branch of the armed forces?

19 Which 15th-century Bible printer is considered to be the inventor of movable type?

20 What "N" is a medical disorder characterized by sudden and uncontrollable attacks of deep sleep?

PREVIOUS TOTAL

125,000

75,000

50,000

25,000

10,000

5,000

2,500

1,000

BANKED

TOTAL

Answers

1	New York Jets.	11	Kato Kaelin.
2	The United Nations.	12	Fish.
3	Audi.	13	Nostradamus.
4	Sherwood Forest.	14	(Male) gigolo.
5	Meat Loaf.	15	Keebler.
6	Christa McAuliffe.	16	Twenty-four.
7	Eleven.	17	*George*.
8	Hazardous Material.	18	(U.S.) Marine Corps.
9	Watt.	19	Johann Gutenberg.
10	Milton Bradley.	20	Narcolepsy.

Round Four

1 In which month does the Mexican holiday Cinco de Mayo occur?

2 In mythology, who was the Greek god of the sea?

3 Which Russian artistic director of the American Ballet Theater starred in the movie *White Nights*?

4 Which American town was the site of a trial and hanging of 19 women thought to be witches in 1692?

5 What English word can describe both a type of fruit pie, and one who mends shoes?

6 In music, T-Boz, Left-Eye, and Chilli are members of what R&B girl group?

7 From the Persian for "waistband," what is the broad, pleated sash worn with a dinner jacket or tuxedo?

8 In movies, which game show was the subject of Robert Redford's Academy Award-nominated film *Quiz Show*?

9 In hobbies, what does a philatelist collect?

10 Which serial killer, known as "The Killer Clown," was executed on May 10, 1994?

11 In the original *Star Trek* television series, which character was played by James Doohan?

12 According to legend, what was the name of Paul Bunyan's blue ox?

13 In geography, eight of the ten highest mountains in the world are found in what country?

14 In movies, which comic actress headlined the film *Superstar*, as schoolgirl Mary Katherine Gallagher?

15 Which computer company was founded in 1976 by Stephen Wozniak and Steven Jobs?

WEAKEST LINK

16 Which San Francisco merchant began his clothing line by selling pants made from tent canvas to California gold miners?

17 Which North Carolina village was the site of the Wright brothers' first flight of a power-driven aircraft?

18 What nickname was legally added to the full name of boxer Marvin Hagler?

19 Which performer has won an Emmy, an Oscar, a Tony and a Grammy: Frank Sinatra or Helen Hayes?

20 What "L" was selected as "Toy of the Century" by *Forbes* magazine?

Answers

1	May.	13	Nepal.
2	Poseidon.	14	Molly Shannon.
3	Mikhail Baryshnikov.	15	Apple Computers.
4	Salem.	16	Levi Strauss.
5	Cobbler.	17	Kitty Hawk.
6	T.L.C.	18	Marvelous.
7	Cummerbund.	19	Helen Hayes.
8	*Twenty-One*.	20	Lego.
9	Stamps.		
10	John Wayne Gacy Jr.		
11	Scotty.		
12	Babe.		

PREVIOUS TOTAL

125,000

75,000

50,000

25,000

10,000

5,000

2,500

1,000

BANKED

TOTAL

Round Five

1 In the Jules Verne classic *20,000 Leagues Under the Sea*, who is the skipper of the submarine *Nautilus*?

2 Which composer and arranger, nicknamed "Q," scored the music for the movie *The Color Purple*?

3 Approximately 30 miles long and home to several million bats, Carlsbad Caverns is located in which state?

4 Is the product known as Canadian Mist a brand of shampoo or whisky?

5 In nature, what "P" is the Malaysian word for an irrigated field where rice is grown?

6 Which tanker spilled over 10 million gallons of crude oil off the coast of Alaska in 1989?

7 In literature, who wrote the novels *From Russia, With Love* and *Goldfinger*?

8 During the Great Depression, which U.S. President gave a series of informal radio addresses known as "Fireside Chats?"

9 In nature, which of the following snakes is venomous: anaconda or copperhead?

10 In food, the pasta shape called "farfalle" is literally the Italian word for which insect?

11 In television, Christopher Hewett played the title character in which sitcom about a British housekeeper?

12 Which television star wrote the New York Times bestselling book, *Leading With My Chin*?

13 Popular in 1830s France, which risqué dance is known for its high kicks that expose the petticoat?

14 In military history, which Nazi Field Marshal was known as "The Desert Fox?"

15 In theater, which playwright wrote *Glengarry Glen Ross*?

WEAKEST LINK

125,000

75,000

50,000

25,000

10,000

5,000

2,500

1,000

BANKED

TOTAL

16 In horse racing, Baltimore's Pimlico Race Course is the home of which Triple Crown Event?

17 In history, what was the name of the second man to walk on the Moon?

18 In architecture, Frank Lloyd Wright designed what New York City museum which opened in 1959?

19 In meteorology, what instrument is used for measuring atmospheric pressure?

20 In geography, how many U.S. states touch the Pacific Ocean?

Answers

1	Captain Nemo.	14	Erwin Rommel.
2	Quincy Jones.	15	David Mamet.
3	New Mexico.	16	Preakness Stakes.
4	Whisky.		
5	Paddy.	17	Edwin "Buzz" Aldrin.
6	Exxon Valdez.		
7	Ian Fleming.	18	The Guggeheim Museum.
8	Franklin Delano Roosevelt.		
9	Copperhead.	19	Barometer.
10	Butterfly.	20	Five.
11	Mr. Belvedere.		
12	Jay Leno.		
13	The Can-can.		

Round Six

1   In cartoons, Yogi Bear and Boo Boo originally inhabited which fictional park?

2   What does the letter "B" stand for in the automobile company B.M.W.?

3   In music, which instrument is Yo-Yo Ma famous for playing?

4   In language, the term "fortnight" refers to how many consecutive days?

5   In medicine, the "R.H. factor" found in red blood cells gets its name from which type of primate?

6   In literature, Napoleon, Snowball and Old Major are characters in which George Orwell novel?

7   In economics, who is the current Chairman of the Board of the U.S. Federal Reserve?

8   In television, what 1970s cop show starred David Soul and Paul Michael Glazer?

9   What dolls, designed by artist, Xavier Roberts were shoppers scrambling to buy in the 1983 Christmas season?

10   In geography, Marblehead is a suburb of which U.S. city: Baltimore or Boston?

11   What President of the National American Woman Suffrage Association appeared on a U.S. dollar coin?

12   In business, name CNN's founder who is known as the "Mouth from the South?"

13   The movies *Get Shorty* and *Out of Sight* were both based on novels by which writer?

14   At the Vatican, when a new Pope is elected, it is announced by a plume of which color smoke?

15   In theater, Oscar Hammerstein wrote the lyrics for the Broadway show *South Pacific*. Who composed the music?

16 What does the "W" in George W. Bush stand for?

17 The "Fat Boy" and the "Hugger" are models produced by which U.S. motorcycle manufacturer?

18 In advertising, which insurance company's slogan tells you to "Get a Piece of the Rock?"

19 Who was the first African-American to be crowned Miss America?

20 In geometry, which type of angle measures greater than 90 degrees but less than 180 degrees?

Answers

1	Jellystone.	11	Susan B. Anthony.
2	Bavaria.	12	Ted Turner.
3	Cello.	13	Elmore Leonard.
4	Fourteen.	14	White.
5	Rhesus Monkey.	15	Richard Rogers.
6	*Animal Farm*.	16	Walker.
7	Alan Greenspan.	17	Harley-Davidson.
8	*Starsky And Hutch*.	18	Prudential.
9	Cabbage Patch Kids.	19	Vanessa Williams.
10	Boston.	20	Obtuse.

Round Seven

1 According to the lyrics of the classic Christmas song. what were Frosty the Snowman's eyes made of?

2 The U.S. Department of Defense's headquarters are located in which Arlington, Virginia building?

3 Who painted "The Creation of Adam" on the ceiling of the Sistine Chapel?

4 *Blubber* and *Superfudge* are both coming-of-age books written by which author?

5 In language, what "K" is a brand of shoe polish, a flightless bird and a fruit?

6 Once the wealthiest man in the world, which American billionaire established an art museum in Malibu, California?

7 In television, which fitness guru stars in his workout videos *Disco Sweat* and *Sweatin' to the Oldies*?

8 In nature, a giant panda's main source of food is derived from which type of woody tropical grass?

9 Which star of the movies *Dead Ringers* and *Lolita* can also be found in print ads for Donna Karan?

10 In history, the Treaty of Guadalupe Hildago established peace between Mexico and which other country?

11 What "A" is an animal composed of only one cell that has no fixed shape?

12 In movies, for which film did Paul Newman win an Academy Award for Best Actor?

13 In sports, which baseball slugger was known as the "Yankee Clipper?"

14 In education, which British university is older: Cambridge or Oxford?

15 What is the two-word motto for the Boy Scouts of America?

16 Which Nobel Prize-winner did *Time* magazine name Person of the Century?

17 Which delivery company is famous for the slogan, "When it absolutely, positively has to be there overnight?"

18 What "O" is the Japanese art of decorative paper folding?

19 In science, which 15th-century Polish astronomer was the first to suggest that Earth orbits the Sun?

20 In geometry, how many total sides are there on a nonagon?

PREVIOUS TOTAL

125,000

75,000

50,000

25,000

10,000

5,000

2,500

1,000

BANKED

TOTAL

Answers

1	Coal.	11	Amoeba.
2	The Pentagon.	12	*The Color of Money.*
3	Michelangelo (di Lodovico Buonarroti Simoni).	13	Joe DiMaggio.
		14	Oxford.
4	Judy Blume.	15	"Be Prepared".
5	Kiwi.	16	Albert Einstein.
6	Jean Paul Getty.	17	Federal Express.
7	Richard Simmons.	18	Origami.
8	Bamboo.	19	Nicolaus Copernicus.
9	Jeremy Irons.	20	Nine.
10	United States.		

Round Eight

1 The Beatles made their American television debut performing on which 1960s variety show?

2 Which dessert—made with Lady Fingers and Espresso—gets its name from the Italian phrase "Pick Me Up?"

3 The Four Gospels of the New Testament are attributed to Matthew, Mark, John, and whom?

4 Which *Guinness Book* record-holder for tap dancing developed the show *Lord of the Dance?*

5 The highest temperature ever recorded on Earth was at the town Aziza on which continent?

6 Trademarked by DuPont in 1946, which coating is used on cooking utensils to prevent sticking?

7 In advertising, which paper towel brand calls itself "The quicker picker-upper?"

8 Which type of steerable balloon airship is named for the German Count who invented it?

9 In politics, which former KGB agent suceeded Boris Yeltsin as President of Russia?

10 In geography, which of the United States is nicknamed the Keystone State?

11 Which Oscar-nominated actor interviewed President Clinton for an *Earth Day 2000* network TV special?

12 In movies, *Scamp's Adventure* is the home video sequel to which Walt Disney animated film?

13 Attributed to an ancient Greek, what is the traditional oath taken by physicians to observe medical ethics?

14 In science, which famous French oceanic explorer invented the aqua-lung?

15 Named in honor of Antoinette Perry, what annual award is given for excellence in theatre?

WEAKEST LINK

16 In periodicals, which American magazine, founded by Jann Wenner, has had Mick Jagger on its cover over 20 times?

17 In business, which Minneapolis company owns the brands Betty Crocker and Cheerios?

18 What "A" is both a loose, knotted scarf and a horse racing track in England?

19 What is the official national language of Brazil?

20 In music, before releasing *Wednesday Morning 3 a.m,* which duo recorded under the alias "Tom and Jerry?

| PREVIOUS TOTAL |
| 125,000 |
| 75,000 |
| 50,000 |
| 25,000 |
| 10,000 |
| 5,000 |
| 2,500 |
| 1,000 |
| BANKED |
| TOTAL |

Answers

1	*The Ed Sullivan Show.*	12	*Lady And The Tramp.*
2	Tiramisu.	13	Hippocratic Oath.
3	(Saint) Luke.	14	Jacques Cousteau.
4	Michael Flatley.	15	Tony Award.
5	Africa.	16	*Rolling Stone.*
6	Teflon.	17	General Mills.
7	Bounty.	18	Ascot.
8	Zeppelin.	19	Portuguese.
9	(Vladimir) Putin.	20	(Paul) Simon and (Art) Garfunkel.
10	Pennsylvania.		
11	Leonardo Di Caprio.		

Round Nine

1   Named for a Swiss doctor, which psychological test is based on interpretations of a series of standard ink blots?

2   In nature, cirrus, nimbus and stratus are all forms of what?

3   In art, Leonardo da Vinci painted the "Mona Lisa" in which century?

4   In math, what "P" is a fraction or ratio with 100 as the denominator?

5   Which rival circus duo did the Ringling Brothers buy out in 1907?

6   In history, JFK's assassin, Lee Harvey Oswald, was in turn shot by whom?

7   In language, a word or phrase that reads the same forward and backward is known as a what?

8   Which actress is married to *Ally McBeal* creator David E. Kelley?

9   In sports, which city hosts horse racing's Kentucky Derby?

10 What is the name of the U.S. Navy's six-jet precision flying team?

11 In movies, which Japanese film-maker directed the movie *Rashamon*?

12 What "P" is the interactive robotic toy dog manufactured by Tiger Electronics?

13 Modern U.S. dimes are made of nickel and which other metallic element?

14 In nature, heroin and opium are derived from the seedpods of which type of flower?

15 In fashion, which New York socialite's designer jean label featured a swan as an emblem?

16 In television, which comic duo did Michael McKean and David L. Lander play on *Laverne and Shirley*?

17 Which camera introduced by Eastman Kodak in 1900 was originally sold for one dollar?

18 In music, which R&B girl group went multi-platinum in the U.S. with their top-ten album *Funky Divas*?

19 How many squares are on the playing surface of a standard chessboard?

20 Meaning "house of bread" in Hebrew, which town is believed to be the birthplace of Jesus Christ?

Answers

1	Rorschach (Test).	11	Akira Kurosawa.
2	Clouds.	12	Poo-Chi.
3	Sixteenth.	13	Copper.
4	Percentage.	14	Poppy.
5	Barnum and Bailey.	15	Gloria Vanderbilt.
6	Jack Ruby.	16	Lenny and Squiggy.
7	Palindrome.		
8	Michelle Pfeiffer.	17	Brownie.
9	Louisville.	18	En Vogue.
10	The Blue Angels.	19	Sixty-four.
		20	Bethlehem.

PREVIOUS TOTAL

125,000

75,000

50,000

25,000

10,000

5,000

2,500

1,000

BANKED

TOTAL

Round Ten

1 What "F" is a strategy used in the U.S. Senate to delay or prevent voting on proposed legislation?

2 By what professional name was film legend Julius Marx better known?

3 In business, what table salt company features an image of a girl with an umbrella on its package?

4 On television's *Frasier*, which actress plays physical therapist Daphne Moon?

5 In holidays, which U.S. Federal Observance occurs on the last Monday in May?

6 Named for its creator, what "M" is a type of bed that folds up inside a wall or closet?

7 In professional tennis, which is the only Grand Slam event currently played on clay?

8 In movies, Oprah Winfrey starred in the film adaptation of which Toni Morrison book?

9 In medicine, which Latin term describes the stiffening of muscles after death?

10 The day after the 1948 Presidential election, the *Chicago Daily Tribune* ran what inaccurate headline?

11 In literature, who wrote the definitive beat novel titled *On the Road*?

12 In beverages, what "G" is an Italian brandy distilled from post-pressed grape residue?

13 In music, the 2001 Grammy for Best New Artist went to which female country music veteran?

14 According to Norse mythology, what "V" is where warriors go when they die?

15 In fashion, the material cashmere is derived from the wool of which animal?

16 Which Microsoft billionaire owns the NFL's Seattle Seahawks and NBA's Portland Trailblazers?

17 What red crested finch is the state bird of seven different states?

18 In religion, which Irish plant did St. Patrick use to illustrate the Holy Trinity?

19 In history, which country fought a war against Great Britain over the Falkland Islands?

20 In television, which network produces and airs the programs *Behind the Music* and *Storytellers*?

Answers

1	Filibuster.	12	Grappa.
2	Groucho (Marx).	13	Shelby Lynne.
3	Morton (Salt).	14	Valhalla.
4	Jane Leeves.	15	Goat.
5	Memorial Day.	16	Paul Allen.
6	Murphy.	17	The Cardinal.
7	The French Open.	18	Shamrock.
8	*Beloved.*	19	Argentina.
9	"Rigor mortis."	20	VH–1.
10	Dewey defeats Truman.		
11	Jack Kerouac.		

Round Eleven

1 What "P" is the temple of the goddess Athena, found on the Acropolis?

2 In science, 32 degrees Fahrenheit is equal to which temperature on the Celsius scale?

3 Puccini's opera *La Boheme* was the basis for which 1996 Tony Award-winning Broadway musical?

4 A spelunker is one who makes a hobby of exploring and studying what?

5 In business, Jeff Bezos is the CEO and founder of e-commerce website?

6 Awarded to soldiers wounded or killed in action, the medal known as the Purple Heart carries the image of which U.S. President?

7 How many sequels have been made to the Mel Gibson/Danny Glover movie *Lethal Weapon*?

8 In literature, Salman Rushdie was sentenced to death by Ayatollah Khomeini for writing which book?

9 In television, Horshack, Boom Boom, and Epstein were regular characters on what 1970s sitcom?

10 In science, physicist Edwin Land founded which instant film and camera company?

11 In pop music, who is the lead singer of the Irish band U2?

12 Name the Catholic nun who won the 1979 Nobel Peace Prize for her work in Calcutta?

13 In movies, which 1973 Al Pacino film about police corruption was based on a real-life story?

14 In literature, which 1851 epic novel begins with the words, "Call me Ishmael?"

15 On December 11, 1941, Germany and which other nation declared war on the United States?

WEAKEST LINK

16 Born Betty Joan Perske, what was the stage name of Humphrey Bogart's fourth and last wife?

17 The Genesis and the Dreamcast game consoles were both produced by which video game company?

18 In geography, which of the United States is known as the Cornhusker State?

19 The word "Dynamo" is an anagram for which day of the week?

20 Which Scottish-born steel baron wrote *The Gospel of Wealth* and established a New York Concert Hall?

Answers

1	Parthenon.	12	Mother Teresa.
2	Zero (nought).	13	Serpico.
3	*Rent.*	14	*Moby Dick.*
4	Caves.	15	Italy.
5	Amazon.com.	16	Lauren Bacall.
6	George Washington.	17	Sega.
7	Three.	18	Nebraska.
8	*The Satanic Verses.*	19	Monday.
9	*Welcome Back, Kotter.*	20	Andrew Carnegie.
10	Polaroid.		
11	Bono.		

Round Twelve

1 In advertising, what Proctor and Gamble deodorant uses the slogan "Strong enough for a man, but made for a woman?"

2 In math, what is the cube root of one thousand?

3 What 984-foot tall structure served as the gateway to the Paris International Exposition of 1889?

4 In television, Trey Parker and Matt Stone created which animated cartoon series that debuted in 1997?

5 In movies, which director received Oscar nominations for both *Traffic* and *Erin Brockovich* in the same year?

6 In tennis, name the Williams sister who won the 2000 Wimbledon singles title?

7 In which month does the American holiday Father's Day occur?

8 The U.S. Navy's "Tailhook Scandal" involved a convention of naval aviators gathered in what city?

9 In art, what "F" is a mural painted with watercolors on moist plaster?

10 In baseball, which Baltimore Orioles short-stop broke Lou Gehrig's record for consecutive games played?

11 Which of the following vegetables is a tuber: Potato or Cabbage?

12 Name the *Friends* actress who also appeared in the original video for Bruce Springsteen's song "Dancin' in the Dark?"

13 In computer language, what does the acronym F.A.Q. stand for?

14 In anatomy, which is the largest bone in the human body?

15 Which international organization, established by the Treaty of Versailles, was disbanded in 1946?

16 In television, for which HBO drama series did actor James Gandolfini win an Emmy Award?

17 In music, what 1996 Latin dance hit was penned by Los Del Rio?

WEAKEST LINK

18 In which state would you find Microsoft's Redmond headquarters?

19 Which Oscar-winning actress was the three-year-old bare-bottomed "Coppertone Girl?"

20 Made from the fermented juice of the agave plant, what type of distilled liquor is named for a town in Mexico?

PREVIOUS TOTAL

125,000

75,000

50,000

25,000

10,000

5,000

2,500

1,000

BANKED

TOTAL

Answers

1	Secret.	12	Courtney Cox (Arquette).
2	Ten.	13	Frequently Asked Questions.
3	The Eiffel Tower.		
4	South Park.	14	Femur.
5	Steven Soderbergh.	15	League of Nations.
6	Venus.	16	*The Sopranos.*
7	June.	17	(The) Macarena.
8	Las Vegas.		
9	Fresco.	18	Washington.
10	Cal Ripken, Jr.	19	Jodie Foster.
11	Potato.	20	Tequila.

Round Thirteen

1 Monica Lewinsky and Jerry Mathers have both appeared in ads for which weight-loss company?

2 Which musician was awarded the National Humanities Medal for his efforts to preserve Walden Woods?

3 In literature, which author wrote *The Hunchback of Notre Dame?*

4 What "J" is the ballet company that performed to the pop music of Prince in its production titled "Billboards?"

5 Which is the most common metallic element found in the earth's crust?

6 In language, what is the literal English translation of the festival called Mardi Gras?

7 In government, the 107th U.S. Congress is comprised of how many senators?

8 In movies, which character in *The Wizard of Oz* wants a brain?

9 From the Greek for "measured journey," which automobile instrument displays the number of miles travelled?

10 Actor Clint Eastwood was once the mayor of which California city: Monterey or Carmel?

11 In the TV series *The Honeymooners* what was the last name of Ralph Kramden's buddy played by Art Carney?

12 In Science, what single-celled fungi causes bread to rise and beer to ferment?

13 In religion, which holy city do devout Muslims turn toward in prayer five times a day?

14 In their music video, what new-wave band performed their song "Whip It" while wearing red plastic hats?

15 Which Ohio school was the first U.S. college to be co-ed and to confer degrees on women?

WEAKEST LINK

16 What art of arranging furniture to aid the flow of "chi" means "wind water" in Chinese?

17 What actor starred in *The Hudsucker Proxy*, *The Hustler* and *Hud*?

18 In business, which worldwide hamburger chain originally sold their "Whopper" for just 37 cents?

19 Which of the Seven Wonders of the Ancient World stood in the harbor at Rhodes?

20 In business, what woman has been chief executive of Playboy Enterprises since 1988?

125,000

75,000

50,000

25,000

10,000

5,000

2,500

1,000

BANKED

Answers

1	Jenny Craig.	14	Devo.
2	Don Henley.	15	Oberlin College.
3	Victor Hugo.		
4	Joffrey Ballet.	16	Feng shui.
5	Aluminum.	17	Paul Newman.
6	Fat Tuesday.	18	Burger King.
7	One hundred.	19	The Colossus.
8	The Scarecrow.	20	Christie Hefner.
9	Odometer.		
10	Carmel.		
11	(Ed) Norton.		
12	Yeast.		
13	Mecca.		

TOTAL

Round Fourteen

1 Founded in 1955, what is the largest tax preparation company in the United States?

2 In television, which fictional Cincinnati radio station featured disc jockeys Venus Flytrap and Dr. Johnny Fever?

3 In math, how many sides are there to a rhombus?

4 The Verrazano-Narrows bridge connects two counties within which U.S. city?

5 Which 1998 H.B.O. movie chronicled the famous celebrity clique that included Frank Sinatra and Dean Martin?

6 In astronomy, which British scientist was the first to calculate the orbit of a comet?

7 In literature, who wrote the once banned book *Tropic of Cancer*?

8 What Winter Olympics event is a combination of cross-country skiing and rifle-shooting?

9 What American composer wrote the music for the original "Rhapsody in Blue"?

10 In history, a cow belonging to what woman was blamed for starting the Great Chicago Fire of 1871?

11 Which international film festival, held each May on the French Riviera, awards the Palme d'Or?

12 What "E" is a branch of medicine dealing with hormones and glands?

13 For more than 100 years, what U.S. city has been home to the annual Mummer's Parade?

14 What famous New York disco was opened by Steve Rubell and Ian Schrager in 1977?

15 Edam, Jarlsberg and Fontina are all types of which food?

16 What Japanese company was the first to market the quartz watch?

17 Which Egyptian president shared the 1978 Nobel Peace Prize with Menachem Begin?

18 Which is a purplish color: puce or teal?

19 Who is the current U.S. Secretary of Defense?

20 Overlooking the Potomac River, what is the name of George Washington's estate and burial place?

PREVIOUS TOTAL

125,000

75,000

50,000

25,000

10,000

5,000

2,500

1,000

BANKED

TOTAL

Answers

1	H & R Block.	12	Endocrinology.
2	WKRP (in Cincinnati).	13	Philadelphia.
		14	Studio 54.
3	Four.	15	Cheese.
4	New York City.	16	Seiko.
5	*The Rat Pack.*	17	Anwar Sadat.
6	Edmund Halley.	18	Puce.
7	Henry Miller.	19	Donald Rumsfeld.
8	Biathlon.		
9	George Gershwin.	20	Mount Vernon.
10	Mrs. O'Leary.		
11	Cannes Film Festival.		

Round Fifteen

1 In television, what former star of *NYPD Blue* got his start playing the son of a tycoon on *Silver Spoons*?

2 In fashion, what "D" is a hat named for the British earl who founded an annual horse race?

3 The 747 Jumbo Jet was first manufactured by which American aerospace company?

4 In movies, what remake of *Thunderball* brought Sean Connery back to the role of James Bond after 12 years?

5 Businessman Sam Walton opened the first of what national chain of discount stores in Rogers, Arkansas?

6 Approximately every hour, the geyser known as Old Faithful erupts in what national park?

7 In math, a nanosecond is what fraction of a second?

8 What "Tech-war" novelist was also a commercial spokesperson for Priceline.com?

9 What Japanese currency is also an English word for "longing?"

10 In politics, which Rhodes Scholar and Clinton advisor published his memoir titled *All Too Human*?

11 Johnny Knoxville is the masochistic host of what MTV show?

12 In geography, what artificial waterway connects the Great Lakes with the Hudson River?

13 What talk show host established *O* magazine in the year 2000?

14 In military history, Japan signed the terms of surrender for World War II aboard what American battleship?

15 In movies, who played William Shakespeare in the 1998 film *Shakespeare In Love*?

16 The alimentary canal is part of which human anatomy system: circulatory or digestive?

WEAKEST LINK

17 What Houston, Texas, based girl group has had hits with the songs "No, No, No" and "Bills, Bills, Bills?"

18 What novel by John Steinbeck follows the Joad family during the Great Depression?

19 What Paris art museum was once called the Musée Napoléon?

20 In mythology, what Roman god of love was the son of Venus?

PREVIOUS TOTAL

125,000

75,000

50,000

25,000

10,000

5,000

2,500

1,000

BANKED

TOTAL

Answers

1	Rick Schroeder.	11	*Jackass.*
2	Derby.	12	Erie Canal.
3	Boeing.	13	Oprah Winfrey.
4	*Never Say Never Again.*	14	The *Missouri.*
		15	Joseph Fiennes.
5	Wal-Mart.	16	Digestive.
6	Yellowstone Park.	17	Destiny's Child.
7	One billionth.	18	*The Grapes of Wrath.*
8	William Shatner.	19	The Louvre.
9	Yen.	20	Cupid.
10	George Stephanopolous		

Round Sixteen

1. What four-word motto was added to U.S. coins in 1864?

2. In geography, what Asian capital is home to the "Forbidden City?"

3. What "D" is a type of camel that has only one hump?

4. In basketball, what seven-foot-tall Los Angeles Laker superstar was known as "The Big Dipper" and "The Stilt?"

5. "It's everywhere you want to be," is the slogan of what credit card company?

6. In movies, which 1988 film garnered Tom Hanks his first Best Actor Oscar nomination?

7. In music, who wrote the lyrics to "The Star Spangled Banner?"

8. In television, Blossom, Bubbles and Buttercup are the main characters of what animated cartoon series?

9. In the landmark 1954 U.S. Supreme Court case, Brown sued the Board of Education of what Kansas city?

10. What Russian ballet star was the subject of the 1972 movie *I Am A Dancer*?

11. In industry, what German auto company's name literally means "people's car?"

12. In 1989, which U.S. Lieutenant Colonel was convicted for his role in the Iran-Contra Affair?

13. Which actress has been married to members of both Bon Jovi and Motley Crue: Pamela Anderson or Heather Locklear?

14. In theater, Irish playwright Samuel Beckett's *Waiting For Godot* was originally written in what language?

15. In movies, what "W" is the fictional species to which the *Star Wars* character Chewbacca belongs?

16. What country music singer spent a brief stint playing with the San Diego Padres during 1999 spring training?

WEAKEST LINK

17 In the animal kingdom, what is the fastest bird on land?

18 In literature, how many ghosts visit Ebeneezer Scrooge in the Charles Dickens novel *A Christmas Carol*?

19 In movies, what is the last name of the Clint Eastwood character Dirty Harry?

20 In medicine, what family-founded hospital in Rochester, Minnesota, treats more than 200,000 patients every year?

PREVIOUS TOTAL

125,000

75,000

50,000

25,000

10,000

5,000

2,500

1,000

BANKED

TOTAL

Answers

1	In God We Trust.	12	Oliver North.
2	Beijing.	13	Heather Locklear.
3	Dromedary.	14	French.
4	Wilt Chamberlain.	15	Wookiee.
5	Visa.	16	Garth Brooks.
6	*Big*.	17	Ostrich.
7	Francis Scott Key.	18	Four.
8	*Powerpuff Girls*.	19	Callahan.
9	Topeka.	20	Mayo Clinic.
10	Rudolf Nureyev.		
11	Volkswagen.		

Round Seventeen

1 In history, who was the only U.S. President to be sworn into office on an airplane?

2 In sports, Ukrainian Sergei Bubka has broken the world record 35 times in which track-and-field event?

3 In theater, who wrote the plays *Our Town* and *The Matchmaker*?

4 What East Coast state is nicknamed the Garden State?

5 In television, Leonardo DiCaprio played a homeless teen on which family sitcom?

6 Introduced in 1981, which stainless-steel sports car shares its name with the man who created it?

7 In theatre, which writer's plays include *Lost in Yonkers* and *The Odd Couple*?

8 In music, which country singer rose from obscurity in 1957 with the song "Walkin' After Midnight?"

9 In computer terminology, which is larger gigabyte or megabyte?

10 In movies, what 1972 film contained the line, "I'm gonna make him an offer he can't refuse."?

11 According to the Bible, what did God tell Moses to remove when He spoke at the Burning Bush?

12 In history, the Civil War battle known as Antietam, took place in which U.S. state?

13 What General-Mills cereal contains stars and clovers, and claims to be "Magically Delicious?"

14 In *The Iliad*, Paris awarded the the golden apple to what goddess of love?

15 In literature, what journalist wrote the book *Fear and Loathing in Las Vegas*?

WEAKEST LINK

16 What "H" is both a unit of frequency and a rental car company?

17 In astronomy, the North Star is located within what constellation?

18 Which magazine was published first: *Time* or *Newsweek*?

19 In television, Ricky Martin played a singing bartender on what American soap opera?

20 In nature, what frog larva is distinguished by its rounded body and long tail?

PREVIOUS TOTAL

125,000

75,000

50,000

25,000

10,000

5,000

2,500

1,000

BANKED

TOTAL

Answers

1	Lyndon (Baines) Johnson.	13	Lucky Charms.
2	Pole vault.	14	Aphrodite.
3	Thornton (Niven) Wilder.	15	Hunter S. Thompson.
4	New Jersey.	16	Hertz.
5	*Growing Pains.*	17	The Little Dipper.
6	DeLorean.	18	*Time.*
7	Neil Simon.	19	*General Hospital.*
8	Patsy Cline.	20	Tadpole
9	Gigabyte.		
10	*The Godfather.*		
11	His shoes.		
12	Maryland.		

Round Eighteen

1 Which United Nations agency was the principal force in eradicating smallpox?

2 The leaf featured on the current Canadian flag is from which type of tree?

3 In music, who was the original lead singer of Black Sabbath?

4 In politics, who did President George W. Bush appoint as U.S. Secretary of State when he first came into office?

5 In movies, who directed the film *Schindler's List*?

6 In history, Kublai Kahn's victory over the Sung Dynasty gave him control of what country?

7 In math, what is 125 divided by five?

8 What Hasbro military action figure got its name from a Robert Mitchum film?

9 In language, what two-word French phrase translates to "have a good journey?"

10 Which early American patriot invented bifocal glasses: Benjamin Franklin or Betsy Ross?

11 From the Greek meaning "to steal," what psychological term describes a person addicted to theft?

12 In television, who was the original host of *The Twilight Zone*?

13 On February 2, 2000, George W. Bush campaigned at what controversial South Carolina school?

14 What packaged food is advertised as "The San Francisco Treat?"

15 In literature, the ship *Hispaniola* appears in what 1883 Robert Louis Stevenson novel?

16 In art, what "I" is the movement most closely associated with French artists Monet and Renoir?

17 In geography, which river has the greater volume of water: the Amazon or the Nile?

18 Started in 1992, which record label is owned by music icon Madonna?

19 At the end of World War II, what U.S. Army general presided over the surrender of Japan?

20 What brother of Shirley MacLaine won an Academy Award for directing the film *Reds*?

Answers

1	World Health Organization.	11	Kleptomaniac.
2	Maple tree.	12	Rod Serling.
3	Ozzy Osbourne.	13	Bob Jones University.
4	Colin (Luther) Powell.	14	Rice-a-roni.
5	Steven Spielberg.	15	*Treasure Island*.
6	China.	16	Impressionism.
7	Twenty-five.	17	Amazon.
8	GI Joe.	18	Maverick.
9	Bon voyage.	19	General Douglas MacArthur.
10	Benjamin Franklin.	20	Warren Beatty.

PREVIOUS TOTAL

125,000

75,000

50,000

25,000

10,000

5,000

2,500

1,000

BANKED

TOTAL

Round Nineteen

1 What brand of canvas high-top sneakers are also known as "Chuck Taylors?"

2 In fashion, what "K" is a loose, wide-sleeved traditional Japanese robe?

3 What 1970s song by Van McCoy started a dance step by the same name?

4 To protest British taxation, rebellious Americans tossed 342 chests of tea into Boston Harbor in 1773?

5 What former world champion boxer was also nominated for a 2001 Grammy Award?

6 Named for a British estate which Olympic sport is played with a shuttlecock?

7 On *The Bullwinkle Show*, what was the name of the boy adopted by Mr. Peabody the Dog?

8 Which large amphitheatre in Rome was opened in 80 A.D. to showcase gladiator combat?

9 In which month of the year do Americans observe Presidents' Day?

10 What island nation was ruled by "Papa Doc" and "Baby Doc" Duvalier?

11 In music, what "La Bamba" singer was posthumously inducted into the Rock and Roll Hall of Fame?

12 What "H" is the unit of measurement used to determine the height of a horse?

13 What train that ran from Paris to Istanbul was the subject of an Agatha Christie mystery?

14 In movies, what 1970s comedy duo starred in the film *Up In Smoke*?

15 In marine biology, what do the letters in the acronym SCUBA stand for?

16 In theater, which Italian opera term literally means "First Lady?"

17 In technology, when measuring heat quantity, what do the initials B.T.U. stand for?

18 In sports, who is the only player to have played in both the World Series and the Super Bowl?

19 In U.S. currency, how many nickels make up one dollar?

20 The Muslim holy city of Mecca is located in which country?

125,000
75,000
50,000
25,000
10,000
5,000
2,500
1,000

BANKED

Answers

1	Converse.	14	Cheech and Chong.
2	Kimono.		
3	"The hustle."	15	Self-Contained Underwater Breathing Apparatus.
4	Tea.		
5	Oscar de la Hoya.		
6	Badminton.	16	Prima donna.
7	Sherman.	17	British Thermal Unit.
8	Colosseum.		
9	February.	18	Deion Sanders.
10	Haiti.	19	Twenty.
11	Ritchie Valens.	20	(Kingdom of) Saudi Arabia.
12	Hand.		
13	*Orient Express.*		

TOTAL

Round Twenty

1 In radio, which music format has the most registered stations in the United States: jazz or country?

2 In U.S. measurements, how many inches are in a linear yard?

3 In television, the theme song of what sitcom was Gary Portnoy's "Where Everybody Knows Your Name?"

4 In mythology, how many eyes did the cyclops have?

5 Huey and Earl Long were both governors of which U.S. state?

6 What planet is known as both the morning star and the evening star?

7 Which singer teamed up with Mariah Carey to record the *Prince of Egypt* soundtrack single "When You Believe?"

8 Which Spanish actress played Matt Damon's love interest in the movie *All The Pretty Horses?*

9 Founded in Kansas City in 1928, the letters F.F.A. stand for the future members of which American profession?

10 In psychology, triskadekaphobia is the abnormal fear of what number?

11 In nature, what winter shrub—popular during the Christmas season—is named for an American diplomat?

12 Which former *Cosmopolitan* magazine editor wrote the book *Sex and the Single Girl?*

13 In the comic strip *Peanuts*, what breed of dog is Snoopy: basset hound or beagle?

14 Engineer Richard James unintentionally invented which children's springy toy?

15 A millennial anniversary marks the passing of how many years?

16 The flag of which North African nation is entirely green?

17 What 1994 Playboy Playmate of the Year was the co-host of MTV's *Singled Out?*

18 What World War II European recovery program was named for the Secretary of State who proposed it?

19 What "S" is an Arabic word for "journey," and describes an exploration or hunting expedition?

20 In geography, what "V" is the longest river in Europe?

PREVIOUS TOTAL

125,000

75,000

50,000

25,000

10,000

5,000

2,500

1,000

BANKED

TOTAL

Answers

1	Country.	13	Beagle.
2	Thirty-six.	14	Slinky.
3	*Cheers.*	15	One thousand.
4	One.	16	Libya.
5	Louisiana.	17	Jenny McCarthy.
6	Venus.	18	Marshall Plan.
7	Whitney Houston.	19	Safari.
8	Penelope Cruz.	20	Volga.
9	Farmers.		
10	Thirteen.		
11	Poinsettia.		
12	Helen Gurley Brown.		

Round Twenty-One

1 For nearly fifty years, Arthur Fiedler directed which contemporary offshoot of the Boston Symphony Orchestra?

2 Which actress portrayed real-life zoologist Diane Fossey in the movie *Gorillas in the Mist*?

3 According to Hoyle, in a standard game of cribbage a player wins by pegging how many points?

4 The "Last Stand" of George Custer occurred during which battle, named for a Montana territory river?

5 What infomercial King teamed up with his father to create and sell the "Veg-o-Matic?"

6 In food, which tiny rice-shaped pasta takes its name from the Italian word for barley?

7 What trademarked line of underwear was founded in 1876 by partners Bradley, Vorhees and Day?

8 Since 1863, the U.S. holiday of Thanksgiving has always fallen on which day of the week?

9 In science, the process of heating milk to remove harmful bacteria was named for which French chemist?

10 In geography, which northwestern English city was birthplace to all four of the Beatles?

11 The children's building toys known as Lincoln Logs were invented by the son of what American architect?

12 In television, which NBC sitcom features the coffee-house called Central Perk?

13 In literature, *The Canterbury Tales* were written by which 14th-century English poet?

14 Since 1969, what brand of pet food has used a spokes-cat named Morris?

WEAKEST LINK

15 What Junk-Bond king received a ten-year jail sentence for securities fraud in 1990?

16 In music, what fictional TV pop band performed the 1970 hit song "I Think I Love You?"

17 In movies, which Quaid brother is the star of the film, *The Big Easy*: Dennis or Randy?

18 How many letters are in the modern Roman alphabet?

19 Named for a state in Mexico, what is the smallest recognized breed of dog?

20 Which car-maker, known for its G.T. model, was taken over by Ferrari in 1997?

Answers

1	The Boston Pops	12	*Friends.*
2	Sigourney Weaver.	13	Geoffrey Chaucer.
3	121.	14	Nine Lives.
4	(The battle of) Little Bighorn.	15	Michael R. Milken.
5	Ron Popiel.	16	The Partridge Family.
6	Orzo.	17	Dennis.
7	B.V.D.	18	Twenty-six.
8	Thursday.	19	Chihuahua.
9	Louis Pasteur.	20	Maserati.
10	Liverpool.		
11	Frank Lloyd Wright.		

PREVIOUS TOTAL

125,000

75,000

50,000

25,000

10,000

5,000

2,500

1,000

BANKED

TOTAL

Round Twenty-Two

1   What overstuffed sandwich is named for a character in the comic strip *Blondie*: Dudley or Dagwood?

2   In medicine, which emergency maneuver named for a Cincinnati surgeon is used to treat choking victims?

3   What machine did *Time* magazine name as its "Man of the Year" for 1982?

4   On television's *Diff'rent Strokes*, what was the name of Arnold's older brother, played by Todd Bridges?

5   In sports, which Canadian province is the home of the Calgary Stampede?

6   For devouring a plague of locusts in 1848, the Mormons built a monument to which type of coastal bird?

7   In geography, what is the capital of Illinois?

8   In Music, what singer dropped the nickname "Little" before his song "Superstition" became a number one hit?

9   In advertising, "Have It Your Way" was the slogan for which major fast food chain?

10 Which amendment to the U.S. Constitution abolished slavery?

11 In the movie *Gone With the Wind*, what is the name of Scarlett O'Hara's plantation home?

12 What couple who wrote the book *The Human Sexual Response*, divorced after 21 years of marriage

13 In politics, John McCain is a Senator representing what Grand Canyon state?

14 Which comic strip by Russell Myers features a buzzard, a troll and a cigar-chomping witch?

15 In international affairs, what do the letters in NATO stand for?

16 Started in 312 B.C., the historic road known as the Appian Way is located in what country?

17 Which former school teacher founded the American Red Cross?

18 In television, what former *Today* show host became the first female network news anchor?

19 What is the only current U.S. state capital that ends with the letter "X?"

20 In business, what national chain is named after the first mate in Herman Melville's *Moby Dick*?

Answers

1	Dagwood.	13	Arizona.
2	Heimlich.	14	Broom-Hilda.
3	Computer.	15	North Atlantic Treaty Organization.
4	Willis.		
5	Alberta.	16	Italy.
6	Seagull.	17	Clara Barton.
7	Springfield.	18	Barbara Walters.
8	Stevie Wonder.	19	Phoenix.
9	Burger King.	20	Starbucks.
10	Thirteenth Amendment.		
11	Tara.		
12	Masters & Johnson.		

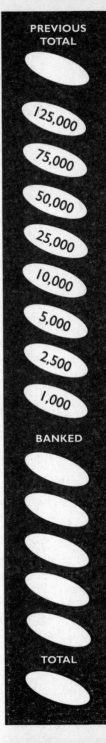

PREVIOUS TOTAL

125,000

75,000

50,000

25,000

10,000

5,000

2,500

1,000

BANKED

TOTAL

Round Twenty-Three

1 In plants, the process of converting light energy into chemical energy is known as what?

2 In history, what first name has been shared by the most U.S. presidents?

3 In art, which painter created the 1930 portrait entitled "American Gothic?"

4 What international language school was founded in Rhode Island by a German immigrant in 1878?

5 In movies, of all the Best Picture Oscar winners since 1975, which film has had the shortest title?

6 Which children's board game features the Gumdrop Pass and Lollipop Woods?

7 In medicine, hepatitis is a disease of what human organ?

8 What "H" is a container used for keeping cigars properly moist?

9 In music, what blind pianist recorded the 1960 hit "Georgia On My Mind?"

10 Also known as the Astro Light, what psychadelic 1960s collectible was created by Edward Walker?

11 In which John Steinbeck novel does George tell Lenny about the rabbits?

12 On the TV show *Seinfeld*, what is the name of the character played by Wayne Knight?

13 What two-word pen-name is used by American etiquette expert Judith Martin?

14 What long, pointed animal tooth shares its name with a Fleetwood Mac album?

15 Founded in 1878, what legal organization provides law school accreditation?

16 What singer was backed by The Heartbreakers on his song "Don't Do Me Like That?"

17 In math, to what power is a number raised if it is cubed?

18 In May 2000, which country celebrated the birth of its one billionth citizen?

19 What dark red cherry was named for a Chinese gardener in Oregon?

20 In television, what does the title of the show *C.S.I.* stand for?

125,000

75,000

50,000

25,000

10,000

5,000

2,500

1,000

BANKED

TOTAL

Answers

1	Photosynthesis.	13	Miss Manners.
2	James.	14	*Tusk*.
3	Grant Wood.	15	American Bar Association (ABA).
4	Berlitz.		
5	*Rocky*.	16	Tom Petty.
6	Candyland.	17	Three (third).
7	Liver.	18	India.
8	Humidor.	19	Bing (Cherry).
9	Ray Charles.	20	Crime Scene Investigation.
10	Lava Lamp (Lite).		
11	*Of Mice And Men*.		
12	Newman.		

Round Twenty-Four

1 In Greek mythology, Jason sailed with the Argonauts in search of the Golden What?

2 What author wrote *The Call of the Wild*?

3 The ads of what fast food chain featured a Chihuahua saying "Drop the Char-lupa?"

4 In movies, what Baltimore native wrote and directed *Pink Flamingos*?

5 From the Spanish for "Kill," what bullfighting figure is the man appointed to kill the bull?

6 The name of what U.S. city is Spanish for "City of Angels?"

7 In music, Elton John teamed up on a 2001 concert tour with which Bronx-born piano man?

8 Since 1966, Jerry Lewis has hosted a Labor Day telethon to fight what disability?

9 In U.S. horse racing, the term "Place" describes a horse finishing in which of the top three spots?

10 In history, Richard The Lion-Heart, was king of what country: France or England?

11 In television, Cookie Monster originally appeared on which P.B.S. program?

12 In theatre, which legendary Spanish lover was introduced in the drama *The Seducer of Seville*?

13 In which movie did George Clooney make a cameo appearance: *Saving Private Ryan* or *The Thin Red Line*?

14 Before Apollo, what NASA program launched 12 two-man spacecraft into orbit?

15 What "D" is a Scott Adams comic strip that follows the life of an office computer programmer?

16 Before switching to the convertible Mustang, Barbie drove which Chevrolet sports car?

17 What Chicago Bulls shooting guard was named the NBA's "Most Valuable Player" five times?

18 In television, what correspondent for *60 Minutes Two* also hosts his own talk show on P.B.S.?

19 What actor is married to Sarah Jessica Parker?

20 What form of therapeutic massage gets its name from the Japanese meaning "finger pressure?"

Answers

1	Fleece.	14	Gemini (Project).
2	Jack London.	15	*Dilbert.*
3	Taco Bell.	16	Corvette.
4	John Waters.	17	Michael Jordan.
5	Matador.	18	Charlie Rose.
6	Los Angeles.	19	Matthew Broderick.
7	Billy Joel.	20	Shiatsu.
8	Muscular dystrophy.		
9	Second.		
10	England.		
11	*Sesame Street.*		
12	Don Juan.		
13	*The Thin Red Line.*		

PREVIOUS TOTAL

125,000

75,000

50,000

25,000

10,000

5,000

2,500

1,000

BANKED

TOTAL

Round Twenty-Five

1 In movies, who played "Bond Girl" Dr. Christmas Jones in *The World Is Not Enough*?

2 At 1,149 feet what Las Vegas tower is the tallest building west of the Mississippi River?

3 *Turn On, Tune In, Drop Out* is a book written by which LSD guru?

4 What abundant earth liquid is known as "H_2O?"

5 In a 1986 TV special, David Copperfield magically passed through the stones of what Chinese landmark?

6 Which frequent Mickey Rooney co-star was Liza Minelli's mother?

7 In fashion, what "F" is the Italian sports apparel company endorsed by tennis star Jennifer Capriati?

8 In medicine, what listening device derives its name from the Greek for "Chest?"

9 What actress played Al Pacino's love interest in the film *Frankie & Johnny*

10 On the TV show *Providence*, which profession is practiced by Sydney Hansen: law or medicine?

11 In which month does the U.S. holiday Columbus Day occur?

12 In Music, what "L" is the name B.B. King gave to his trademark Gibson guitar?

13 In geography, the Balkan Peninsula includes which country: Bulgaria or Latvia?

14 Sony features a series of video games starring a bandicoot named what?

15 April, June, September and what other month have a total of thirty days?

WEAKEST LINK

16 To celebrate the first reading of the Declaration of Independence, what was rung on July 8, 1776?

17 In language, the term "smog" is a combination of what two words?

18 In music, "Anarchy In The U.K." was the first single from what Johnny Rotten band?

19 Invented by a German chemist, laboratory burner mixes gas with air to produce a smokeless flame?

20 Who was the second woman appointed to the United States Supreme Court?

Answers

1	Denise Richards.	12	Lucille.
2	Stratosphere (Tower).	13	Bulgaria.
		14	Crash
3	Timothy Leary.	15	November.
4	Water.	16	Liberty Bell.
5	Great Wall of China.	17	Smoke and Fog.
6	Judy Garland.	18	The Sex Pistols.
7	Fila.	19	Bunsen (Burner).
8	Stethoscope.	20	Ruth (Bader) Ginsburg.
9	Michelle Pfeiffer.		
10	Medicine.		
11	October.		

Round Twenty-Six

1 In television, what former talk-show host is married to Marlo Thomas?

2 In math, which of these is a prime number: thirty-one or fifty-one?

3 In the U.S. Military, the Apache and the Chinook are both types of which of aircraft?

4 What hormone secreted by the pancreas lowers blood glucose levels in diabetic patients?

5 In 1973, what 10 year-old actress became the youngest winner of a major Academy Award?

6 In geography, what country is officially known as the Hellenic Republic?

7 In astrology, February 29th falls under what sign of the zodiac?

8 Latin for "to entrust", what legal term means to seclude a jury from outside contact?

9 In music what is the real name of the New Orleans trumpeter known as "Satchmo?"

10 On November 19, 1863, what speech, dedicating a national cemetery, was delivered by President Lincoln?

11 Until 1994, Jane Pratt edited what alternative magazine for teenage girls?

12 In nature, what insect gets its name from the Spanish term for "little fly?"

13 In television, Bob Keeshan starred in what classic children's series that featured Mr Greenjeans?

14 What Republican from Mississippi is the Senate Majority Leader?

15 Which type of earring does corporate mascot Mr Clean wear: a Hoop or a Stud?

16 What radio host and author of *Private Parts* proclaimed himself the "King of All Media?"

17 In American history, what "M" was a band of colonial militia-men that agreed to offer their service at a moment's notice?

18 What American author wrote the 1978 novel *The World According to Garp*?

19 What TV evangelist defrauded followers of his PTL Ministry for $158 million

20 Lou Reed was a member of what rock band whose first album featured a banana on the cover?

PREVIOUS TOTAL

125,000

75,000

50,000

25,000

10,000

5,000

2,500

1,000

BANKED

TOTAL

Answers

1	Phil Donahue.	13	*Captain Kangaroo.*
2	Thirty-one.	14	Trent Lott.
3	Helicopter.	15	Hoop.
4	Insulin.	16	Howard Stern.
5	Tatum O'Neal.	17	Minute Men.
6	Greece.	18	John Irving.
7	Pisces (the fish).	19	Jim Bakker.
8	Sequester.	20	Velvet Underground (And Nico).
9	Louis Armstrong		
10	Gettysburg Address.		
11	*Sassy.*		
12	Mosquito.		

Round Twenty-Seven

1 Who was the first driver to win the Indianapolis 500 four times?

2 What 1976 film popularized the line "I'm mad as hell, and I'm not going to take it anymore!"?

3 James Caan and Billy Dee Williams starred in what 1971 TV movie about a dying football player?

4 In theater, Cordelia, Goneril and Regan are daughters of which Shakespearean title character?

5 The natural oil lanolin comes from the fleece of what species of animal?

6 Robert De Niro and Sandra Bernhard play kidnappers in what 1983 movie?

7 In human biology, which blood type is the most common: type A or type O?

8 Members of which NFL team created the dance called "The Super Bowl Shuffle?"

9 In literature, what horror author created the film series *Hellraiser*?

10 What is the name of the Elvis Presley home in Memphis, Tennesee?

11 Which continent has a larger land area: Antarctica or Australia?

12 What physicist's second law of motion states that "force equals mass multiplied by acceleration?"

13 What actor played Jim Rockford in the television series *The Rockford Files*?

14 In automobiles, what "D" is the graduated rod for measuring the amount of oil in a crank-case?

15 Which New Jersey city is the birthplace of Frank Sinatra?

16 Which member of Buffalo Bill's Wild West Show was a Sioux Indian leader during Custer's last stand?

17 Who recorded the Oscar-winning song "Things Have Changed" for the movie *Wonder Boys*?

18 Which Baldwin brother is older: Alec or Stephen?

19 In 1871, reporter Henry Stanley was sent to Africa to search for what Scottish explorer?

20 What British entrepreneur sold his Virgin Music Group to Thorn EMI for nearly one billion dollars?

Answers

1	A.J. Foyt (Jr).	13	James Garner.
2	*Network*.	14	Dipstick.
3	*Brian's Song*.	15	Hoboken.
4	*King Lear*.	16	Sitting Bull (Tatanka Iyotake).
5	Sheep.		
6	*The King of Comedy*.	17	Bob Dylan
7	Type O.	18	Alec.
8	Chicago Bears.	19	David Livingstone.
9	Clive Barker.		
10	Graceland.	20	(Sir) Richard Branson.
11	Antarctica.		
12	(Sir) Isaac Newton.		

Round Twenty-Eight

1 Which Roger Kahn baseball book shares its title with a Grammy-winning Don Henley song?

2 Named for a New York City hotel, which American Kennel Club held its first annual Dog Show in 1877?

3 Chuck Barris hosted what bizarre game and talent show that debuted in 1976?

4 Which country does the equator pass through: Colombia or Nigeria?

5 According to the U.S. Flag Code, what is the preferable method for disposing of worn-out American flags?

6 Hennessy and Rémy Martin are both types of what French brandy?

7 In which Steven Spielberg-directed TV movie is Dennis Weaver pursued by a killer truck?

8 Which U.S. company is named for the man who created the electric shaver?

9 Yankee Stadium is located in which New York City borough?

10 What is the largest denomination of U.S. Currency currently issued for circulation by the Department of Treasury?

11 What extinct volcano thought to be the final resting place of Noah's Ark is the highest peak in Turkey?

12 Known for his surprise endings, what was the pen name of American short-story writer William Sydney Porter?

13 What portable audio system, sold in the U.S. by Sony, was originally marketed as the "Soundabout?"

14 In geography, what is the only U.S. State with a one-syllable name?

15 In its 89 years of existence, which pocket-sized magazine has never run a cigarette ad?

16 In history, Leslie Lynch King, Jr. was the birth name of what U.S. president?

17 In language, what French term for a dead-end street literally means "bottom of the bag?"

18 What Chinese-born American architect designed the Rock and Roll Hall of Fame?

19 Prior to 1954, what was Veterans' Day called in the U.S.?

20 According to *Billboard*, the members of which boy band were the first artists born in the 1980s to have a song reach Number One?

Answers

1	*The Boys of Summer*.	13	Walkman.
2	Westminster.	14	Maine.
3	*The Gong Show*.	15	*Reader's Digest*.
4	Colombia.	16	Gerald Ford.
5	Burning.	17	Cul de sac.
6	Cognac.	18	I.M. (Ieoh Ming) Pei.
7	*Duel*.	19	Armistice Day.
8	Schick.	20	Hanson.
9	The Bronx.		
10	$100 bill		
11	Mount Ararat (Agri Dagi).		
12	O. Henry.		

PREVIOUS TOTAL

125,000

75,000

50,000

25,000

10,000

5,000

2,500

1,000

BANKED

TOTAL

Round Twenty-Nine

1. In the *Batman* comic books, the alter-ego of which villain is named Edward Nigma?

2. What North American marsupial has fifty teeth, more than any other land mammal?

3. From 1932 to 1998, what word appeared above Washington's head on U.S. quarters?

4. In history, what name was given to the B–29 aircraft that dropped the atomic bomb on Hiroshima?

5. In music, what rock band recorded an album with the San Francisco Symphony titled *S & M*?

6. In the Clement C. Moore poem "Twas the Night Before Christmas," which of Santa's reindeer is the last one mentioned?

7. Which second son of Eric the Red is thought to have reached North America almost 500 years before Christopher Columbus?

8. What sports drink did Professor Robert Cade originally develop for the University of Florida football team?

9. In politics, what man was the Speaker of the U.S. House of Representatives before stepping down in 1998?

10. In the Second Punic War what general crossed the Alps with elephants to attack Italy?

11. In history, what was the number of the first manned Apollo mission to land on the Moon?

12. In geography, what volcano is the highest mountain in Japan?

13. What athletic endurance competition gets its name from the site of a Greek battle about 25 miles outside Athens?

14. In medicine, what drug company trademarked the name "aspirin" in 1899?

15. The official languages of Tanzania are English and what language?

WEAKEST LINK

16 What U.S. magazine is published by and named for the institution that runs 16 museums and the US National Zoo?

17 According to its Latin name, the constellation Ursa-Major depicts what type of animal?

18 Which peanut-filled candy bar was named after the Mars family's favorite horse?

19 In a Vice-Presidential debate, which candidate told Dan Quayle "Senator, you're no Jack Kennedy."?

20 In literature what 17th-century scholar wrote the epic poem "Paradise Regained" as a sequel to his "Paradise Lost"?

Answers

1	The Riddler.	12	Mt Fuji (Fujiyama).
2	Possum (Opossum).	13	Marathon.
3	Liberty.	14	Bayer.
4	*Enola Gay*.	15	Swahili.
5	Metallica.	16	Smithsonian.
6	Blitzen.	17	Great Bear.
7	Leif Eriksson.	18	Snickers (bar).
8	Gatorade.	19	Senator Lloyd Bensen.
9	Newt Gingrich.		
10	Hannibal.	20	John Milton.
11	Apollo XI (eleven).		

PREVIOUS TOTAL

125,000

75,000

50,000

25,000

10,000

5,000

2,500

1,000

BANKED

TOTAL

Round Thirty

1 Which species is the tallest land mammal in the animal kingdom?

2 What city is home to the U.S. Supreme Court building?

3 What Mexican food item literally translates to "little donkey?"

4 In movies, which 1980s comedy spawned sequels subtitled *Mission to Moscow* and *Citizens on Patrol*?

5 In astronomy, what planet of our solar system is known for its great red spot?

6 The characters Inky, Pinky, Blinky and Clyde first appeared in which Atari video game?

7 Which U.S. company became the first to retail a line of frozen foods?

8 What "M" is the style of Mexican music featured on a 1987 Linda Ronstadt album?

9 Which U.S. coin featured a portrait of a bison on its reverse side from 1913 to 1938?

10 In television, which NBC show premiered first: *Friends* or *Frasier?*

11 In roman numerals, what calendar year is represented by the letters MM?

12 In astrology, what is the term for the transition point between two signs of the zodiac?

13 In movies, what Australian actor plays the title role in the *Crocodile Dundee* films?

14 If it is 3.00p.m. in New York City, what time is it in Detroit, Michigan?

15 In music, what veteran rock band released the album *Just Push Play?*

16 What is the four-word title of Hillary Clinton's 1996 best-selling book?

17 What is the only U.S. state name that ends with the letter "K"?

18 In television, which actress played *Dr. Quinn, Medicine Woman*?

19 With more than 43 million members. which North American organization is the world's largest motor club?

20 What unit of land-measurement equals 43,560 square feet?

Answers

1 Giraffe.	14 Same time (3.00 pm).
2 Washington D.C.	
	15 Aerosmith.
3 Burrito.	16 *It Takes A Village.*
4 *Police Academy.*	17 New York.
5 Jupiter.	18 Jane Seymour.
6 Pac Man.	19 AAA (Triple A).
7 Birds Eye	20 Acre.
8 Mariachi.	
9 (Buffalo) Nickel.	
10 *Frasier.*	
11 2000.	
12 Cusp.	
13 Paul Hogan.	

PREVIOUS TOTAL

125,000

75,000

50,000

25,000

10,000

5,000

2,500

1,000

BANKED

TOTAL

Round Thirty-One

1 Founded by Cecil Rhodes, what "D" is the world's largest diamond company?

2 In movies, the title of a 1963 film featured King Kong battling what giant Japanese monster?

3 Inspired by a Tony Orlando song, what color ribbons were worn during the Iranian hostage crisis?

4 What year is the next leap year?

5 What movie-inspired nickname did the media give to Ronald Reagan's missile defense system?

6 Omaha, Kansas City and Sioux City all lie on which American river?

7 Which national bus company issues the North America Discovery Pass?

8 Christina Applegate first played promiscuous Kelly Bundy on what Fox sitcom?

9 In music, Yusuf Islam originally released the song "Moonshadow" under which name?

10 Mozart composed his operas in Latin, German and which other language?

11 In sports, before joining the Lakers, Shaquille O'Neal played for which other NBA team?

12 In movies, what film, based on a comic book about an all-girls rock band, starred Rachel Lee Cook?

13 The Australian National University is located in what capital city?

14 What was the code name for Woodward and Bernstein's secret Watergate source?

15 Noted for howling at night, the prairie wolf is better known by what Aztec name?

16 The Bastille Opera House is located in what European city?

17 What backward-gliding dance step is the title of Michael Jackson's autobiography?

18 What Kenneth Grahame children's novel follows the adventures of Mole, Rat, Toad and Badger?

19 In television, what city was the setting for the drama series *Homicide: Life on the Street?*

20 On the most recent *Fortune 500* list what is the highest-ranking corporation whose name starts with an "X?"

PREVIOUS TOTAL

125,000

75,000

50,000

25,000

10,000

5,000

2,500

1,000

BANKED

TOTAL

Answers

1	De Beers.	12	*Josie And The Pussycats.*
2	*Godzilla (Gojira).*	13	Canberra.
3	Yellow.	14	Deep Throat.
4	2004.	15	Coyote.
5	*Star Wars.*	16	Paris.
6	Missouri.	17	*Moonwalk.*
7	Greyhound.	18	*The Wind In The Willows.*
8	*Married With Children.*	19	Baltimore.
9	Cat Stevens.	20	Xerox.
10	Italian.		
11	Orlando (Magic).		

Round Thirty-Two

1 In music, which character was represented in the group The Village People: A firefighter or a construction worker?

2 In fashion, what company's jeans logo is a triangle with a question mark?

3 Which U.S. city is home to the Whitney Museum of American Art?

4 Found in a trench in France, what German shepherd dog went on to star in more than twenty Hollywood films?

5 What group of Ecuadorian islands was named for the giant tortoises that inhabit it?

6 In food, what term for ordering separately priced items is French for "by the menu?"

7 In sailing, what "S" is the nautical term for the rear end of a boat?

8 In music, which Latin rock pioneer won a Grammy with Rob Thomas for the song "Smooth?"

9 In 1988, Chrysler became the first U.S. automaker to include what safety device as standard equipment?

10 Which California city is home to the Tournament of Roses parade?

11 Before he escaped and returned to France, Napoleon Bonaparte was exiled to what island?

12 In television, which actress plays Dana Scully on *The X Files*?

13 Which day of the week comes first alphabetically?

14 In 1935, the "Trial of The Century" focused on the kidnapping of which famed aviator's baby?

15 In math, what Greek letter is used to express the ratio of the circumference of a circle to its diameter?

WEAKEST LINK

16 What 1952 John Steinbeck novel is based on the biblical story of Cain and Abel?

17 In geography, Port of Spain is the capital of Trinidad and which other island?

18 Which country singer recorded a pop album under the guise of fictional character Chris Gaines?

19 In anatomy, which sense organ contains the anvil and stirrup bones?

20 After a dispute with President Truman, which General was removed from his command of the Korean War?

Answers

1	Construction worker.	12	Gillian Anderson.
2	Guess.	13	Friday.
3	New York (City).	14	Charles Lindbergh.
4	Rin Tin Tin.	15	Pi.
5	Galapagos (Islands).	16	*East Of Eden*.
6	A la carte.	17	Tobago.
7	Stern.	18	Garth Brooks.
8	Carlos Santana.	19	(Middle) Ear.
9	Air bag.	20	Douglas MacArthur.
10	Pasadena.		
11	Elba.		

Round Thirty-Three

1 The Greek servant Damocles was forced to sit while what item was suspended over his head?

2 In Television, Pamela Anderson had an early role as a "Tool Time" Girl on what sitcom?

3 After the *Santa Maria* sank, on which ship did Columbus return to Europe from his first voyage to America?

4 During Prohibition, which Justice Department agent led the unit known as "The Untouchables?"

5 Babett March was the cover girl on the first "Swimsuit Edition" of which magazine?

6 What German car company manufactures models called the Boxster and the Nine-Eleven?

7 Which political party held its 2000 convention at the Staples Center in Los Angeles?

8 In music, what Irish singer tore up a photo of Pope John Paul II on *Saturday Night Live*?

9 Frederick Forsythe's novel, *The Day of the Jackal*, concerns a plot to assassinate the president of what country?

10 John Madden is the spokesman for what chain of stores which offer a "Helpful Hardware" club?

11 In television, what producer of *Hill Street Blues* was also responsible for the police musical *Cop Rock*?

12 In geography, what modern country was known as Persia until 1935?

13 In the Old Testament, while fleeing the destruction of Sodom and Gomorrah, Lot's wife was turned into what?

14 Which restaurant chain first used the phrase "Pizza! Pizza!" in 1979?

WEAKEST LINK

15 In which movie does Jimmy Stewart star as a man who befriends a giant, invisible Rabbit?

16 Which British Prime Minister won the 1953 Nobel Prize for Literature?

17 In horse racing, which Triple Crown-winner has the fastest time in Kentucky Derby history?

18 In music, which Beatle sang lead vocals on the song "Yellow Submarine?"

19 In an adult what curved structure of the human back has a total of 26 bones?

20 What early-model Ford automobile was nicknamed the "Tin Lizzie?"

125,000

75,000

50,000

25,000

10,000

5,000

2,500

1,000

BANKED

Answers

1	Sword.	12	Iran
2	*Home Improvement*	13	Salt (Pillar of Salt).
3	*Nina.*	14	Little Caesar's.
4	Eliot Ness.	15	*Harvey.*
5	*Sports Illustrated.*	16	Winston Churchill.
6	Porsche.	17	Secretariat.
7	Democrat Party.	18	Ringo Starr.
8	Sinead O'Connor.	19	Spine.
9	France.	20	Model T.
10	Ace.		
11	Steven Bochco.		

TOTAL

Round Thirty-Four

1. In television, Corky Sherwood and Jim Dial were regular characters on which series?

2. Which Ohio native wrote the classic western, *Riders of the Purple Sage*?

3. What European Principality is home to the world-famous casino in Monte Carlo?

4. Bip is the alter-ego of what French mime artist known for his classic work "Walking Against the Wind?"

5. Brook, Dolly Varden and Rainbow are species of which fish?

6. Which celebrity has been married more times: Larry King or Elizabeth Taylor?

7. During the Civil War, what iron-clad ship engaged in battle with the *Merrimack*?

8. From the Latin for "ornamental gardening," what is the art of trimming trees into animals and other odd shapes?

9. What is the professional name of the Australian supermodel born Eleanor Gow?

10. In medicine, the ailment known as conjunctivitis is also refered to by what colorful name?

11. What Virginia village was the site of the first permanent English settlement in the United States?

12. With moves like "the elbow spin," which street-dance gave its name to a 1984 Joel Silberg film?

13. In money, which country uses the dollar as its basic unit of currency: Bolivia or Hong Kong?

14. What British actor played Captain Picard on *Star Trek: The Next Generation*?

15 Which U.S. President proclaimed the first Sunday following Labor Day as National Grandparents Day?

16 Which "Science Guy" suggested that NASA's *Surveyor* carries a sundial to Mars?"

17 In literature, what is the name of the young protagonist in *The Catcher In the Rye*?

18 From 1971 to 1997, the Democratic Republic of the Congo was called what?

19 Which country music trio had a hit with "Goodbye Earl?"

20 What word refers to both a thin loaf of French bread and a rectangular-cut gemstone?

PREVIOUS TOTAL

125,000

75,000

50,000

25,000

10,000

5,000

2,500

1,000

BANKED

TOTAL

Answers

1	*Murphy Brown.*	13	Hong Kong.
2	Zane (Pearl) Grey.	14	Patrick Stewart.
		15	Jimmy Carter.
3	Monaco.	16	Bill Nye.
4	Marcel Marceau.	17	Holden Caulfield.
5	Trout.	18	Zaire.
6	Elizabeth Taylor.	19	Dixie Chicks.
7	The *Monitor.*	20	Baguette.
8	Topiary.		
9	Elle McPherson.		
10	Pink-eye.		
11	Jamestown.		
12	Breakdancing.		

Round Thirty-Five

1   In movies, which professional wrestler played the role of the Scorpion King in *The Mummy Returns*?

2   Infantry, Cavalry, and Artillery cards are key to which 1959 Parker Brothers game of world conquest?

3   In music, what pop singer's 2001 album was titled *J. Lo*?

4   During the Monica Lewinsky scandal, which Pentagon employee told the American people "I am you"?

5   In television, "Conjunction Junction" and "I'm Just A Bill" were part of which Saturday-morning series of animated shorts?

6   In math, when multiplying two negative numbers is the result a negative or a positive?

7   In language, what Turkish word for "fate" is also the title of a Broadway musical?

8   What newspaper word game was invented by Arthur Wynne for the *New York World*?

9   In sports, which golfer is the youngest to ever win the Masters: Jack Nicklaus or Tiger Woods?

10   In geography, which National park is home to the lowest elevation in the Western Hemisphere?

11   In literature, what authors novels include *The Time Machine* and *The Invisible Man*?

12   In the animal kingdom, the young of which long-necked bird is called a cygnet?

13   Is Romanian a Slavic language or a Romance language?

14   In tennis, Billie Jean King won the "Battle of the Sexes" match by beating what male opponent?

15   What daily newspaper was founded in 1889 by Charles H. Dow and Edward Jones?

16 While visiting a Trenton, New Jersey school, former Vice-President Dan Quayle famously misspelled what word?

17 What country artist and sausage-company owner sang the hit song "Big Bad John?"

18 Gardner Cowles founded what picture magazine in 1937 to compete with *Life*?

19 What Indiana University has a football team named the Boiler-makers?

20 What brand of gin, first made in 1820, was named for the Tower of London guards who protected the royal Crown Jewels?

Answers

1	The Rock (Dwane Johnson).	**11**	H.G. Wells.
2	Risk.	**12**	Swan.
3	Jennifer Lopez.	**13**	Romance.
4	Linda Tripp.	**14**	Bobby Riggs.
5	*Schoolhouse Rock.*	**15**	*Wall Street Journal.*
6	Positive.	**16**	Potato.
7	Kismet.	**17**	Jimmy Dean.
8	Crossword Puzzle.	**18**	*Look.*
9	Tiger Woods.	**19**	Purdue.
10	Death Valley.	**20**	Beefeater.

PREVIOUS TOTAL

125,000

75,000

50,000

25,000

10,000

5,000

2,500

1,000

BANKED

TOTAL

Round Thirty-Six

1 When facing Mount Rushmore, which President's head is farthest to your left?

2 In 1960, which Soviet premier stunned the United Nations by banging his shoe on the table?

3 In 1940, what candy company introduced its Peppermint Pattie?

4 The name of what building used for gambling comes from the Italian word for "house?"

5 What kind of teenage monster was portrayed by Michael Landon in a 1957 film?

6 In biology, how many cells does an amoeba have?

7 In Music, what band had a Number One hit in 1970 with the song "A.B.C.?"

8 In the light spectrum, what do the letters U.V. stand for?

9 In anatomy, skeletal, smooth, and cardiac are the three basic types of what tissue?

10 Julia Roberts won an Academy Award for her portrayal of which legal campaigner?

11 In 1878, a legendary feud began between the Hatfields and what Kentucky family?

12 What documentary film about the 1992 Clinton presidential campaign was nominated for an Oscar?

13 What musical instrument is pictured in the logo of Guinness beer?

14 In geography, the 49th Parallel is an imaginary line dividing the United States from what country?

15 From the French for "sitting," what is a meeting where people attempt to speak with the dead?

WEAKEST LINK

16 In music, which woodwind instrument has a double reed: the basset horn or the bassoon?

17 In literature, who wrote about his experiences in professional football in the book *Paper Lion*?

18 According to the U.S. Constitution, no one may be elected President more than how many times?

19 In math, what is 69 divided by three?

20 What New York nightclub founded by Sherman Billingsley used a logo of a long-necked bird with a top hat?

PREVIOUS TOTAL

125,000

75,000

50,000

25,000

10,000

5,000

2,500

1,000

BANKED

TOTAL

Answers

1	George Washington.	11	McCoy (family).
2	Nikita Khruschchev.	12	*The War Room.*
3	York (Cone Co).	13	Harp.
		14	Canada.
4	Casino.	15	Seance (session).
5	Werewolf.	16	Bassoon.
6	One.	17	George Plimpton.
7	The Jackson Five.	18	Two.
8	Ultraviolet.	19	Twenty-three.
9	Muscle (muscular).	20	Stork Club.
10	Erin Brockovich.		

Round Thirty-Seven

1 The first name of which *Ally McBeal* actress is Greek for "most beautiful?"

2 What official flower of Mother's Day was called Jove's Flower by the Romans?

3 What Egyptian star of *Lawrence of Arabia* wrote a newspaper column about bridge?

4 The Michael Moore film *Roger & Me* focused on auto plant closings in what Michigan city?

5 Commercials for what brand of audio-tape featured a singer shattering a glass with her voice?

6 Which American revolutionary figure became synonymous with the word traitor by forming an allegiance with Britain?

7 What athletic shoe manufacturer took its name from the Greek goddess of victory?

8 What men's magazine uses the slogan "The Best Thing to Happen to Men Since Women?"

9 Which day of the week gets its name from the Norse god of thunder?

10 In sports, what did the NBA's Washington Bullets change their name to in 1997?

11 In television, the highest-rated program of all time was the final episode of what series?

12 Campaigning for her husband in 1976, who endeared herself to truckers by using the CB handle "First Mama?"

13 In Shakespeare's *Romeo and Juliet*, was Romeo a Capulet or a Montague?

14 What British passenger liner crossed the Atlantic 1001 times before permanently docking in Long Beach, California?

WEAKEST LINK

15 Which New York borough was originally called New Amsterdam?

16 The name for an eagle's sharp claw comes from which French word for "heel?"

17 What "D" is a dark chamber used to confine prisoners?

18 In music, what was the name of the lead singer of the Grateful Dead leader who died in 1995?

19 The book *Our National Parks* features the work of which nature photographer?

20 When strong light is shined on the human eye does the pupil expand or contract?

125,000

75,000

50,000

25,000

10,000

5,000

2,500

1,000

BANKED

Answers

1	Calista (Flockhart).	11	*M*A*S*H*.
2	(Pink) Carnation.	12	Betty (Elizabeth) Ford.
3	Omar Sharif.	13	Montagu.
4	Flint.	14	*Queen Mary*.
5	Memorex.	15	Manhattan.
6	Benedict Arnold.	16	Talon.
7	Nike.	17	Dungeon.
8	*Maxim*.	18	Jerry Garcia.
9	Thursday.	19	Ansel Adams.
10	Washington Wizards.	20	Contract.

TOTAL

Round Thirty-Eight

1 Who was the first African-American to host his own national late-night television talk-show?

2 Which Popeye cartoon-character is known for saying "I will gladly pay you Tuesday for a hamburger today"?

3 Which Truman Capote book recounts the 1959 murder of a rural Kansas family?

4 Groucho Marx plays the dictator of what fictitious country in the movie *Duck Soup*?

5 What deep shade of red is the school nickname of Harvard University's sports teams?

6 In children's literature, the character known as "the man with the yellow hat" is the trusted companion of what monkey?

7 In 1994, a Maryland man crashed an airplane onto the lawn of what Washington D.C. building?

8 In music, which singer turned the song "Unforgettable" into a duet with her late father?

9 How long does it take light to travel from the sun to the earth: eight seconds or eight minutes?

10 Tap-dancing star Bill Robinson went by which nickname that was also the title of his biography?

11 Which nation won its independence from European Colonial Powers first: India or Algeria?

12 On television's original *Fantasy Island*, who played the mysterious Mr Roarke?

13 What bookstore chain owns B. Dalton and Doubleday Book Shops?

14 In which European country would you find the port city of Antwerp?

15 In literature, what American poet wrote "I Sing the Body Electric?"

16 Which performer has hosted the Academy Awards more times: Billy Crystal or Bob Hope?

17 What state fruit of Georgia is honored annually with a festival during the month of June?

18 The Intimate Brand company owns what chain of stores known for their lingerie catalogue?

19 According to the American Dairy Association, what is the most popular type of cheese in America?

20 In music, which Madrid-born tenor is the artistic director of the Los Angeles Opera?

PREVIOUS TOTAL

125,000

75,000

50,000

25,000

10,000

5,000

2,500

1,000

BANKED

TOTAL

Answers

1	Arsenio Hall.	12	Ricardo Montalban.
2	(J. Wellington) Wimpy.	13	Barnes & Noble.
3	*In Cold Blood.*	14	Belgium.
4	Fredonia.	15	Walt Whitman.
5	Crimson.	16	Bob Hope.
6	Curious George.	17	Peach.
7	The White House.	18	Victoria's Secret.
8	Natalie Cole.	19	Cheddar.
9	Eight minutes.	20	Placido Domingo.
10	(Mr.) Bojangles.		
11	India.		

Round Thirty-Nine

1 In Literature, which nationally syndicated gossip columnist published a memoir titled *Natural Blonde*?

2 Which sitcom featured a British theatre producer who hires a child care worker played by Fran Drescher?

3 In anatomy, the metacarpals are bones located in which part of the human body?

4 In photography, what term for a camera-stand comes from the Latin for "three-footed?"

5 Which Roman gladiator led a slave revolt that became the subject of a 1960 Kirk Douglas film?

6 William Gray installed the first public coin-operated version of what device at a Connecticut Bank in 1889?

7 In movies, which comedian is the star of the film *Blue Streak*?

8 What term for a philandering ladies man comes from the name of a real life 18th-century Italian lover?

9 In geography, which West Indies country is home to Montego Bay?

10 In law, what "G" is the wooden mallet used by a judge to signal order in the court?

11 In 1984, which female pop star recorded the hit single "Girls Just Wanna Have Fun?"

12 Used in horse-racing, what U.S. customary unit of measurement is equal to one-eighth of a mile?

13 In U.S. military radio communications, which male name is spoken to signify that a message has been received and understood?

14 In television, what was the maiden name of the sisters played by Delta Burke and Dixie Carter on *Designing Women*?

15 In literature, what novel tells the tragic tale of the adulterous puritan Hester Prynne?

WEAKEST LINK

125,000

75,000

50,000

25,000

10,000

5,000

2,500

1,000

BANKED

16 What term from the old English for "oath-breaker" refers to a male witch?

17 First published in Edinburgh, what is the oldest and largest general encyclopedia in the English language?

18 Which star of the film *Oklahoma!* played the mom on *The Partridge Family*?

19 The U.S. Presidents who immediately succeeded Lincoln and Kennedy both had what last name?

20 Which flowering tree shares its name with the title of a Paul Thomas Anderson film?

Answers

1	Liz Smith.	14	Sugar-Baker.
2	*The Nanny.*	15	*The Scarlet Letter.*
3	Hand.		
4	Tripod.	16	Warlock.
5	Spartacus.	17	Encyclopedia Britannica.
6	Telephone.		
7	Martin Lawrence.	18	Shirley Jones.
8	Casanova.	19	Johnson.
9	Jamaica.	20	Magnolia.
10	Gavel.		
11	Cyndi Lauper.		
12	Furlong		
13	Roger.		

TOTAL

Round Forty

1 What "J" is an official national gathering of the Boy Scouts of America?

2 What Lake Tahoe ski resort hosted the 1960 Winter Olympics?

3 Which 31-year-old magazine for African-American women gives its name to a yearly awards show and a July music festival?

4 Which fascist leader ruled Spain from the 1930s until his death in 1975?

5 In television, what 1980s sitcom character was played by Emmanuel Lewis?

6 What term, from the Latin for "enclosed place," refers to an abnormal fear of small spaces?

7 Palermo is the capital of which Mediterranean island?

8 Elsie the cow was the mascot for what brand of milk?

9 The 1996 film *Brain Candy* starred which Canadian comedy troupe?

10 According to the book *The Real Mother Goose*, in the poem *The Cat and the Fiddle*, who did the dish run away with?

11 In the Old Testament, David kills Goliath with a stone flung from what weapon?

12 Earl Anthony and Walter Ray Williams, Jr are superstars in what pro sport?

13 In geography, what country was formerly known as Ceylon?

14 The infamous phrase "Let them eat cake," was attributed to what Queen of France?

15 In technology, which half-inch Sony videotape format was released prior to VHS?

WEAKEST LINK

16 What ABC show became famous for the catch phrase, "The thrill of victory and the agony of defeat?"

17 In theater, which musical is based on a Barry Manilow song about a showgirl named Lola?

18 Which type of whale is the largest of all known animals?

19 In architecture, what gate stands as the arch-of-triumph for the city of Berlin?

20 In movies, what *48 Hours* star received an Oscar nomination for his role in *Affliction*?

125,000

75,000

50,000

25,000

10,000

5,000

2,500

1,000

BANKED

Answers	
1 Jamboree.	12 (Ten-pin) bowling.
2 Squaw Valley.	13 Sri Lanka.
3 *Essence*.	14 Marie Antoinette.
4 Generalissimo (General) Franco.	15 Beta (Betamax).
5 Webster Long.	16 (ABC's) *Wide World of Sports*.
6 Claustrophobia	17 *Copacabana*.
7 Sicily.	18 Blue whale.
8 Borden (Dairy)	19 Brandenburg.
9 Kids in the Hall.	20 Nick Nolte.
10 The Spoon.	
11 Sling (slingshot).	

TOTAL

Round Forty-One

1 What term for elaborate decorative lettering comes from the Greek word for "beautiful writing?"

2 The poet Ogden Nash wrote "candy is dandy but liquor is" what?

3 In 1951, a Houston radio station was the first to transmit traffic reports using what form of airborne transportation?

4 In the song "America the Beautiful," what color are the "mountain majesties?"

5 In the U.S. Constitution, what "Q" is the minimum attendance necessary for Congress to do business?

6 What pair of Disney chipmunks starred in the Oscar-nominated cartoon *Toy Tinkers?*

7 Which newspaper began publishing the Pentagon Papers on June 13, 1971?

8 In television, what actor played inept reporter Matthew on the sitcom, *News-radio?*

9 In colleges, animal mascot is shared by Auburn, Clemson, Princeton and LSU?

10 From the Greek for "forgetfulness," is the medical term for memory loss

11 An Indian word meaning "ship at the end of the rainbow," is Mexico's largest seaside resort?

12 In movies, Gwyneth Paltrow starred in a 1998 film-adaptation of which Charles Dickens' novel?

13 What legendary MGM tap dancer starred opposite Mickey Rooney in the original Broadway cast of *Sugar Babies?*

14 For more 1000 years, which city was the capital of Imperial Japan?

15 In the animal kingdom, which rodent is also known as the quill pig?

16 In literature, which girl detective made her first appearance in the book *The Secret of the Old Clock*?

17 What U.S. city has hosted an NFL game on Thanksgiving Day every year since 1945?

18 What planet in our solar system takes 12 months to complete one orbit of the sun?

19 Using the slogan "Driven," what automaker manufactures the X-terra S.U.V.?

20 In which organ of the human body would you find Broka's area?

Answers

1	Calligraphy.	14	Kyoto.
2	Quicker.	15	Porcupine (hedge-hog/spinehog).
3	Helicopter.	16	Nancy Drew.
4	Purple.	17	Detroit.
5	Quorum.	18	Earth.
6	Chip and Dale.	19	Nissan.
7	*New York Times.*	20	Brain.
8	Andy Dick.		
9	Tiger.		
10	Amnesia.		
11	Cancun.		
12	*Great Expectations.*		
13	Ann Miller.		

PREVIOUS TOTAL

125,000

75,000

50,000

25,000

10,000

5,000

2,500

1,000

BANKED

TOTAL

Round Forty-Two

1 In rock music, which lead singer from the band Hole was married to Kurt Cobain?

2 According to the Gemological Institute of America, the four "C"s of diamond quality are color, clarity, carat-weight and what?

3 In the Russian Orthodox religion, Christmas Day is officially celebrated on the seventh day of which month?

4 What 3-foot, 9-inch actor founded the charity called Little People of America?

5 What German alcoholic beverage contains 56 herbs, roots and spices and has a name that means "Master of the Hunt?"

6 What is the joyless city mentioned in the last line of Ernest Thayer's poem "Casey at the Bat?"

7 One of South Dakota's Black Hills now bears a 90-foot-tall likeness of which Sioux warrior?

8 Located in the West Indies, the island of Hispaniola is divided between the Dominican Republic and which other nation?

9 Taken from a nursery rhyme, what were the first five words recorded by Thomas Edison into his phonograph?

10 The movie *Ghosts of Mississippi* chronicled the legal proceedings in the assassination of which civil rights leader?

11 From the Latin word for "crown," what term refers to the outermost region of the sun's atmosphere?

12 What 1901 play by Anton Chekov features the characters Olga, Masha and Irina?

13 Which Admiral was killed while leading the British fleet in the Battle of Trafalgar?

14 From the Middle English for "Made in imitation," what word refers to fake or forged currency?

WEAKEST LINK

15 What character beckoned "I Want You?" on World War II Army recruiting posters?

16 What George Gershwin folk opera features the residents of Catfish Row?

17 Which auto manufacturer is credited with selling the first cars equiped with lap and shoulder three-point seat belts?

18 Which two South American countries border Ecuador?

19 Which Agatha Christie "whodunnit" has become the world's longest running play?

20 Following the assassination attempt on Ronald Reagan, what then-Secretary Of State declared, "I'm in control here?"

125,000

75,000

50,000

25,000

10,000

5,000

2,500

1,000

BANKED

TOTAL

Answers

1	Courtney Love.	13	Lord (Horatio) Nelson.
2	Cut.	14	Counterfeit.
3	January.	15	Uncle Sam.
4	Billy Barty.	16	*Porgy And Bess.*
5	Jagermeister.	17	Volvo
6	Mudville.	18	Colombia and Peru.
7	Crazy Horse.		
8	Haiti.	19	*The Mousetrap.*
9	Mary had a little lamb.	20	Alexander Haig.
10	Medgar Evers.		
11	Corona (Aureole).		
12	*Three Sisters.*		

Round Forty-Three

1 In music, what song, written by Michael Jackson and Lionel Ritchie hit No. 1 for the charity group USA for Africa?

2 What small French umbrella gets its name from the Latin meaning "shield from the sun?"

3 What Italian luxury liner sank off the coast of Nantucket Island in 1956 after colliding with the *Stockholm*?

4 Which is the best-selling ice cream flavor in the United States?

5 In horseshoe throwing, what is the official term for a horseshoe that encircles the stake?

6 In music, a concertina is which type of instrument: a harp or an accordion?

7 What brand of in-line skates were first developed as a training tool for hockey players?

8 In literature, what European psychoanalyst wrote *The Interpretation of Dreams*?

9 Which comedian played five members of the Klump family. in the film *The Nutty Professor*?

10 In medicine, Barney Clark was the recipient of the first permanent artificial version of what organ?

11 What cone-shaped hat, worn as a punishment, is named for a 13th-century Scottish philosopher?

12 In television, what do the letters "MS" stand for in the cable network MSNBC?

13 What type of sub-machine gun was developed by an Israeli Army officer just after the 1948 Arab-Israeli War?

14 In geography, what is the only U.S. state that shares a border with Maine?

15 In law, which Latin term, meaning "After death," refers to a coroner's examination?

16 Hay fever is caused by an allergy to what powder-like spores produced by plants?

17 Commercials for Chevy trucks featured the song "Like a Rock," by what musician?

18 What brand of candy bar shares its name with the galaxy we live in?

19 In music, which American composer scored the ballet *Billy the Kid*, and wrote *Fanfare for the Common Man*?

20 The first transcontinental telegraph line in the U.S. was built by which company that now deals primarily in wire transfers of money?

Answers

1	"We Are The World."	13	Uzi.
2	Parasol.	14	New Hampshire.
3	The *Stockholm*.	15	Post Mortem.
4	Vanilla.	16	Pollen.
5	Ringer.	17	Bob Seagar.
6	Accordion.	18	Milky Way.
7	Rollerblade.	19	Aaron Copeland.
8	Sigmund Freud.	20	Western Union.
9	Eddie Murphy.		
10	Heart.		
11	Dunce's (Dunce) Cap.		
12	Microsoft.		

PREVIOUS TOTAL

125,000

75,000

50,000

25,000

10,000

5,000

2,500

1,000

BANKED

TOTAL

Round Forty-Four

1 In literature, which English author wrote *Emma* and *Pride and Prejudice*?

2 What brand of canned snack food uses the slogan, "Once you pop, you can't stop?"

3 What "V" is the Hollywood trade newspaper that has been a source of entertainment news since 1905?

4 What eastern U.S. City is the site of Logan International Airport?

5 In television, what sitcom set in a German PoW camp featured a character named Colonel Klink?

6 What 20th century U.S. President had a wife named Mamie?

7 What is the oldest and largest civil rights organization in the U.S.?

8 In geography ,which two countries share the world's longest undefended border?

9 In music, Whitney Houston's No. 1 hit "I Will Always Love You" was written by what country singer?

10 In archery, what "Q" is a portable case for holding arrows?

11 What tractor company is named for the blacksmith who founded it in 1857?

12 In movies, move played Police Chief Martin Brody in *Jaws*?

13 In the 1970s, Jane Fonda's detractors added what Vietnamese capital to her first name?

14 On television's *Full House*, Michelle Tanner was played by twin actresses with what last name?

15 On April 8, 1974, what baseball player broke Babe Ruth's career home-run record?

WEAKEST LINK

16 Created by William Marston, which female superhero has bulletproof bracelets and an invisible airplane?

17 What singer dropped his last name of Hansen and had a hit with the song "Loser?"

18 The Grand Coulee Dam is located on which Washington State river?

19 What Shakespeare play takes place on Prospero's Island?

20 In which 1987 movie did Patrick Swayze declare, "Nobody puts Baby in a corner?"

PREVIOUS TOTAL

125,000

75,000

50,000

25,000

10,000

5,000

2,500

1,000

BANKED

TOTAL

Answers

1	Jane Austen.	10	Quiver.
2	Pringles.	11	John Deere (and Co.).
3	*Variety*.	12	Roy Scheider.
4	Boston.	13	Hanoi.
5	*Hogan's Heroes*.	14	Olsen.
6	Dwight Eisenhower.	15	Henry (Hank) Aaron.
7	NAACP (National Association for the Advancement of Colored People).	16	Wonder Woman.
		17	Beck.
		18	Columbia.
8	U.S.A. and Canada.	19	*The Tempest*.
		20	*Dirty Dancing*.
9	Dolly Parton.		

Round Forty-Five

1 What "E" is the wacky character Jim Varney portrayed in nine movies and numerous TV commercials?

2 What PBS animated character has the trademarked nickname "the big red dog?"

3 Which word used to describe college grounds and buildings. Is Latin for "field?"

4 Which choreographer played dance instructor Lydia Grant in the movie *Fame*?

5 In literature, which Washington Irving character falls asleep and awakens 20 years later?

6 Which adopted son of Claudius was Emperor of Rome when a fire destroyed half the city in 64 A.D.?

7 In music, which "Material Girl" had a hit with "Like a Virgin?"

8 Besides the $10 bill, what is the only current bill of U.S. paper currency not to feature a portrait of a former President?

9 Tommy Hilfiger's fragrance for men has the same name as what Chris Farley movie?

10 Of the world's national flags, which country's features the most stars?

11 For 35 years, the state of Vermont has held an annual festival honoring which type of syrup-producing tree?

12 What is the only animated feature to receive an Academy Award nomination for Best Picture?

13 What name is shared by the most populous cities in both Maine and Oregon?

14 What "O" is a type of tea which means "black dragon" in Chinese?

15 In 1977, a California housewife named Debbie opened the first store of what worldwide cookie chain?

16 In television, who was the crime-solving coroner played by Jack Klugman?

17 Impact, Striker and Soccer Trainer are all varieties of what Wham-O Footbag?

18 In music, which parody artist recorded the songs "Smells Like Nirvana" and "Eat It?"

19 Reintroduced by John F. Kennedy, the highest award given to civilians is known as the Presidential Medal of what?

20 Which actor played a young Indiana Jones in *Indiana Jones and the Last Crusade*?

PREVIOUS TOTAL

125,000

75,000

50,000

25,000

10,000

5,000

2,500

1,000

BANKED

TOTAL

Answers

1	Ernest (P. Worrell).	13	Portland.
2	Clifford.	14	Oolong.
3	Campus.	15	Mrs Fields (Original Cookies).
4	Debbie Allen.		
5	Rip Van Winkle.	16	Quincy.
6	Nero.	17	Hacky-sack.
7	Madonna.	18	Weird Al Yankovic.
8	The $100 bill.		
9	Tommy Boy.	19	Freedom.
10	U.S.A.	20	River Phoenix.
11	Maple.		
12	*Beauty and the Beast.*		

Round Forty-Six

1 The hammerhead, great white, and mako are all species of what kind of fish?

2 In television what show starred Greg Evergan as a young trucker who traveled with a pet chimp?

3 In math, what is 199 plus 199?

4 In geography, Great Britain ceded control of which territory to China in 1997?

5 In January 2001, which branch of the U.S. Military replaced their recruiting slogan, "Be all you can be?"

6 In music, what guitarist was a member of the bands Cream and Derek And The Dominoes?

7 What association, established in 1884, maintains a pure-bred dog registry?

8 In movies, what actress starred as Catherine Tramell in *Basic Instinct?*

9 What "L" is the hand-held magnifying lens used by gemologists and jewelers?

10 In literature, what British writer known for his erotic novels wrote *Lady Chatterley's Lover?*

11 What ancient mountaintop in Israel was the site of the Jews' last stand against the Romans in 73 A.D.?

12 In May 2001, which Vermont Senator announced that he would leave the Republican Party and become an Independent?

13 In television, what Comedy Central show stars Adam Carolla and Jimmy Kimmel?

14 In anatomy, what is the medical term for the roof of the mouth?

15 What European female was the first gymnast to score a perfect 10 in the Olympic Games?

16 What brand of soap, owned by the W.D. Forty Company, has a wrapper depicting a volcano?

17 What five-time Grammy-winner became a spokesperson for the Psychic Friends Network?

18 In the Old Testament, who was the scheming, power-hungry wife of Ahab?

19 In technology, what company manufactures the computer processor known as the Pentium Four?

20 In movies, which former Calvin Klein model starred with Hugh Grant in *Four Weddings and a Funeral*?

Answers

1	Shark.	13	*The Man Show.*
2	B.J. and the Bear.	14	Palate.
3	398.	15	Nadia Comaneci.
4	Hong Kong.	16	Lava.
5	Army.	17	Dionne Warwick.
6	Eric Clapton.	18	Jezebel.
7	American Kennel Club.	19	Intel.
8	Sharon Stone.	20	Andie MacDowell.
9	Loop.		
10	D.H. Lawrence.		
11	Masada.		
12	Jim Jeffords.		

PREVIOUS TOTAL

125,000

75,000

50,000

25,000

10,000

5,000

2,500

1,000

BANKED

TOTAL

Round Forty-Seven

1 In human biology what disk-shaped blood cells are essential for blood clotting?

2 In literature, Edward and Estlin were the first two names of what poet who seldom used capital letters?

3 In food, what "P" is the cut of steak containing both the T-bone and the tenderloin?

4 In television Mary Hart and Bob Goen host what show-business news program?

5 What French General and Revolutionary War hero lends his name the park across the street from the White House?

6 Which Harold Pinter play takes its title from what small elevator used to move food between floors of a building?

7 Which New York alternative weekly paper was co-founded by Norman Mailer?

8 In music, what band had No. 1 hits with the songs "Jive Talkin'" and "You Should Be Dancing?"

9 In chemistry, what letters from the periodic table represent the common salt compound of sodium chloride?

10 From the Italian for "middle," what name is given to the level of theatre seats located on the lowest balcony?

11 Each year, what city in New Mexico hosts the largest Native American art show in the country?

12 In movies, what 1989 baseball film featured the line "If you build it, he will come?"

13 Also known as Denali, what is the highest mountain in North America?

14 "Wendy the Good Little Witch" first appeared in comic books starring what friendly ghost?

15 What sitcom featured supermodel Heidi Klum as the girlfriend of Michael J. Fox?

16 What "A" is the group of toothless mammals known for its long sticky tongue and diet of insects?

17 Which comedian was the original host of *America's Funniest Home Videos*?

18 What name for the surface of an airport runway comes from an 18th-century Scottish engineer?

19 In Astrid Lindgren's books which pig-tailed Swedish girl lives with a horse and an ape?

20 Also known as "Lady Day," which singer toured with the Count Basie Orchestra?

PREVIOUS TOTAL

125,000

75,000

50,000

25,000

10,000

5,000

2,500

1,000

BANKED

Answers

1	Platelets.	13	Mount McKinley
2	e.e. cummings.	14	Casper.
3	Porterhouse.	15	*Spin City*.
4	*Entertainment Tonight*.	16	Anteater (Ant Bear).
5	Lafayette.	17	Bob Saggett
6	Dumb Waiter.	18	Tarmac
7	*Village Voice*.	19	Pippi Longstocking.
8	The Bee Gees.	20	Billie Holiday.
9	NaCl.		
10	Mezzanine.		
11	Santa Fe.		
12	*Field of Dreams*.		

TOTAL

Round Forty-Eight

1 Tanqueray and Bombay-Sapphire are both types of what liquor?

2 In fashion what formal men's jacket and pants ensemble gets its name from a city north of Manhattan?

3 Which actress portrayed the woman whose sister was her daughter in Roman Polanski's *Chinatown*?

4 In Olympic sports, how many innings make up a standard, regulation softball game?

5 Similar to sucrose what milk sugar is produced by nursing mothers?

6 In the U.S. what lake west of the Mississippi has the largest surface area?

7 On the television series *Alice*, at which restaurant did Alice, Vera, and Flo wait on tables?

8 The coastal redwood is a type of what large conifer tree named for a Cherokee Indian?

9 What Marxist revolutionary and author of *My Life*, moved to Mexico after being exiled by Stalin?

10 What Texas blues guitarist, known for "Pride and Joy," died in a helicopter crash in August of 1990?

11 What species of bear is depicted on the logo for the World Wildlife Fund?

12 What now-defunct New York satire magazine featured the column "Separated At Birth?"

13 Located in Malaysia which twin skyscrapers rank as two of the tallest office buildings in the world?

14 Located on Mount Hood in Oregon, the Timberline Lodge was used in which Shelley Duvall horror film?

15 With a total surface area of about 5.4 million square miles, what is the smallest of the world's major oceans?

WEAKEST LINK

16 First released in 1978, what Milton Bradley electronic game challenged players to repeat a pattern of lights and tones?

17 In movies, Sean Penn and Martin Lawrence each starred in films that shared what title?

18 Taken from Article Two of the U.S. Constitution, what is the name of the annual address the President delivers to Congress?

19 Which of the nine known major planets in our solar system comes last in alphabetical order?

20 By agreeing to face Jimmy Carter, who became the first incumbent President to publicly debate his challenger?

Answers

1	Gin.	13	Petronas Towers.
2	Tuxedo.	14	*The Shining.*
3	Faye Dunaway.	15	Arctic Ocean
4	Seven.	16	Simon
5	Lactose (Lactin)	17	*Bad Boys.*
6	Great Salt Lake.	18	State of the Union.
7	Mel's Diner (Mel's).	19	Venus.
8	Sequoia.	20	Gerald Ford.
9	Leon Trotsky.		
10	Stevie Ray Vaughan.		
11	Panda.		
12	*Spy.*		

PREVIOUS TOTAL

125,000

75,000

50,000

25,000

10,000

5,000

2,500

1,000

BANKED

TOTAL

Round Forty-Nine

1 In business, what brand of natural spring water, named for a town near Lake Geneva, bottles one billion litres annually?

2 In 1971, George Harrison and Ravi Shankar staged an all-star concert to benefit what war-torn Asian country?

3 What Washington D.C. memorial had a half-scale replica made in 1996 designed to travel around the U.S.?

4 What "P" is an athletic shoe company that shares its name with a mountain lion?

5 Which G.M. Auto Division produces the Bonneville and the Sunfire?

6 In television, which animated character wears a Mettalica T-shirt: Beavis or Butthead?

7 What "S" is a short stemmed pear-shaped goblet used to serve brandy?

8 In literature, a 1958 Plymouth is the title character of which Stephen King novel?

9 In astrology, which sign of the zodiac is symbolized by the lion?

10 In music, what former 10,000 Maniacs singer recorded the solo album *Tiger-lily*?

11 What term for a gymnast skilled in balance is a combination of the Greek for "high" and "walk?"

12 Dr. Jonas Salk developed the vaccine for what disease known as infantile paralysis?

13 In which 1996 Cohen brothers' film did Frances McDormand play a Minnesota policewoman?

14 In geology, what "A" is the fossilized tree resin used in jewelry?

15 What honorary title often added to the names of lawyers is abbreviated "Esq?"

16 In geography, which island is larger in area: Greenland or Iceland?

17 According to AT&T, what holiday is the busiest for phone calls?

18 In television, Betty Thomas played Lucy Bates on which police drama series?

19 What "P" is a Japanese pinball game that features steel balls bouncing through a maze of nails?

20 Single malt scotch whiskey is distilled in Scotland from which grain?

PREVIOUS TOTAL

125,000

75,000

50,000

25,000

10,000

5,000

2,500

1,000

BANKED

TOTAL

Answers

1	Evian.	12	Polio (Poliomyelitis/ Poliovirus).
2	Bangladesh.		
3	Vietnam Veterans Memorial.	13	*Fargo*.
		14	Amber.
4	Puma.	15	Esquire.
5	Pontiac.	16	Greenland.
6	Beavis.	17	Mother's Day.
7	Snifter.	18	*Hill Street Blues*.
8	*Christine*.	19	Pachinko.
9	Leo.	20	Barley.
10	Natalie Merchant.		
11	Acrobat.		

Round Fifty

1 The University of the Andes is located in what Colombian capital city?

2 In music, which *Baywatch* star was named Germany's most-popular and best-selling artist of 1989?

3 In literature, which Russian-born author wrote *Atlas Shrugged*?

4 Who was the first American astronaut to be launched into space?

5 In politics, how many senators represent each U.S. State?

6 Which actress won an Academy Award for her role in the film *Dead Man Walking*?

7 Invented by David Brewster, what device creates patterns with glass chips viewed through a hand-held tube?

8 In periodicals, who is the wheelchair-bound publisher of *Hustler* magazine?

9 In the opening credits of *The Brady Bunch*, which character appears in the center square?

10 The Hawaiian islands were first named the Sandwich Islands by which European Explorer?

11 Which planet in our solar system has a moon named Triton?

12 Which month of the year has the most letters in its name?

13 What does the "B" in the U.S. military aircraft B-52 stand for?

14 Known as the windpipe, what air passageway in the throat extends from the larynx to the bronchial tubes?

15 Edmund Morris wrote the biography *Dutch* about which U.S. President?

16 What former host of *Talk Soup* played a gay artist in *As Good As It Gets*?

WEAKEST LINK

17 Barret Hansen is the real name of what radio host known for playing parodies and novelty songs?

18 What New York gang-themed musical was composed by Leonard Bernstein?

19 Named for its American inventor, which cross-shaped slotted screw was designed for power Screwdrivers?

20 In music, what American bandleader composed "Stars and Stripes Forever?"

PREVIOUS TOTAL

125,000

75,000

50,000

25,000

10,000

5,000

2,500

1,000

BANKED

TOTAL

Answers

1	Bogota.	11	Nepture.
2	David Hasselhoff.	12	September.
		13	Bomber.
3	Ayn Rand.	14	Trachea.
4	Alan Shepard.	15	Ronald Reagan.
5	Two.	16	Greg Kinnear.
6	Susan Sarandon.	17	Dr. Demento.
7	Kaleidescope.	18	*West Side Story*.
8	Larry Flint.	19	Phillips.
9	Alice (Nelson/maid/ housekeeper)	20	John Philip Sousa.
10	(Capt) James Cook.		

Round Fifty-One

1 In ceramics, what "K" is the type of oven used to fire clay?

2 In comics, which species of bird was the "Bloom County" character Opus?

3 In movies, what actor played James Bond in the film *GoldenEye*?

4 What book by William S. Burroughs was the object of a censorship trial in Boston in 1965?

5 What German airship burst into flames in Lakehurst, New Jersey in 1937?

6 In what TV series did Neil Patrick Harris play the title role of a teenage doctor?

7 What battery company, once called Ever Ready, is known for its pink spokes-bunny?

8 The annual International balloon fiesta is held in what New Mexico city?

9 In music, which class of instrument is the English horn: a woodwind or a brass?

10 Which small, red fruit flavors the brandy known as kirsch?

11 What large open area in central Moscow is bordered by the Kremlin and St. Basil's Cathedral?

12 From the German for "shot," what "S" is a word for skiing straight downhill often in full tuck position?

13 In human anatomy, what muscle runs along the back of the upper arm and extends the forearm?

14 In television, which *Wheel of Fortune* star was once a regular on *Days of our Lives*?

15 If you were playing baccarat in a Las Vegas casino, would you be playing with cards or dice?

16 In time measurement, what do the letters GMT stand for?

17 In the Spanish-American War, Teddy Roosevelt's "rough riders" rallied to the cry, "Remember the" what?

18 The 3M company sells what brand of transparent adhesive invented by Richard Drew in 1930?

19 In math, what is the square root of 49?

20 What two-word Latin phrase, meaning "In the Year of the Lord," is represented by the letters AD?

PREVIOUS TOTAL

125,000

75,000

50,000

25,000

10,000

5,000

2,500

1,000

BANKED

TOTAL

Answers

1	Kiln.	12	Schuss.
2	Penguin.	13	Tricep (Triceps).
3	Pierce Brosnan.	14	Pat Sajak.
4	*Naked Lunch.*	15	Cards.
5	*Hindenburg.*	16	Greenwich Mean Time.
6	*Doogie Howser (MD).*	17	Maine.
7	Energizer.	18	Scotch (Magic) Tape.
8	Albuquerque.	19	Seven (or negative seven).
9	Woodwind.	20	Anno Domini.
10	Cherries.		
11	Red Square (Krasnaya Ploschad).		

111

Round Fifty-Two

1 What "S" is an alphabet-signaling system, based on waving a pair of hand-held flags in a particular pattern?

2 Once called the blister nut, what nut comes from the same family of plants as poison ivy?

3 In music, which country singer married Lisa Hartman and released the album *Killin' Time*?

4 In history, Wyatt Earp befriended Doc Holliday in which south-western Kansas town?

5 In history, which Egyptian queen committed suicide by letting herself be bitten by a venomous asp?

6 In movies, which actress played Rollergirl in the film *Boogie Nights*?

7 What nurse, and recipient of the British Order of Merit, was known as the "Lady of the Lamp?"

8 Which 90-year-old retail catolog was created by an outdoors-man who first offered mail order rubber boots?

9 What founder of Bolshevism is entombed in a glass coffin in Moscow's Red Square?

10 After seven seasons, who gave up his job as sidekick on *Late Night with Conan O'Brien*?

11 The Sultan of which tiny nation on Borneo ranks among the World's richest men?

12 Famous for the phrase "Holy Cow," which broadcaster led the Chicago Cubs' seventh inning stretch for 16 years?

13 The first fully documented performance of what classical dance form dates to Paris in 1581?

14 What singer originally recorded the song "Walking In Memphis?"

15 Meaning "porous bone," what disease, common in elderly women, leads to a curvature of the spine?

16 What "V" is the only OPEC member-nation located in the Western Hemisphere?

17 What 1998 film takes its name from a three-word greeting to AOL subscribers?

18 James Thurber's short story about a daydreaming hero is called *The Secret Life of* whom?

19 In literature, who wrote the novel *Gone With the Wind*?

20 In technology, what computer company manufactures a laptop model called VAIO?

Answers

1	Semaphore.	11	Brunei.
2	Cashew (Acajou).	12	Harry Caray.
		13	Ballet.
3	Clint Black.	14	Marc Cohen.
4	Dodge City.	15	Osteoporosis.
5	Cleopatra.	16	Venezuela.
6	Heather Graham.	17	*You've Got Mail.*
7	Florence Nightingale.	18	Walter Mitty.
		19	Margaret Mitchell.
8	L.L. Bean.	20	Sony.
9	(Vladimir Ilyich) Lenin.		
10	Andy Richter.		

Round Fifty-Three

1 In cartoons, Mickey Mouse had a dog named for which planet?

2 What small carrier attached to a motorcycle shares its name with a brandy cocktail?

3 Guernsey, Holstein and Brown Swiss are all breeds of what species of animal?

4 Named for a Persian ruler, what is a stone building used as a tomb?

5 Founded in 1934, in which famed Harlem theater did Ella Fitzgerald and James Brown both win amateur night contests?

6 Before Alaska and Hawaii became states, what was the 48th state to be admitted to the Union?

7 Which psychedelic pop artist painted a Boeing 777 for Continental Airlines?

8 In the film *Bang the Drum Slowly*, what sport did Robert DeNiro's character play?

9 What Greek letter organization is America's oldest college honors society?

10 What Marvin Hamlisch Broadway musical is about dancers auditioning for a Broadway musical?

11 In human anatomy, what are the two narrow tubes through which an egg passes to the uterus?

12 What TV series featured Robert Wagner and Stefanie Powers as a wealthy couple who solved crimes?

13 Which Hollywood movie studio trademarked the sound of the lion's roar that opens its films?

14 What "K" is a type of carp found in aquariums and backyard ponds?

15 In which country was the artist Pablo Picasso born?

16 In geography, New York City is divided into how many boroughs?

17 What "P" is a triangular optical device that splits white light into a spectrum?

18 Saxophone player Kenneth Gorelick has recorded several multi-platinum albums under what name?

19 In movies, which member of the Fonda family starred in the film *Singles*?

20 The United States Military Academy is located at what New York military post?

125,000

75,000

50,000

25,000

10,000

5,000

2,500

1,000

BANKED

TOTAL

Answers

1	Pluto.	11	Fallopian (Uterine) Tubes).
2	Sidecar.		
3	Dairy cows (cattle).	12	*Hart To Hart*.
4	Mausoleum.	13	MGM.
5	The Apollo Theater.	14	Koi (King) Carp.
6	Arizona.	15	Spain.
7	Peter Max.	16	Five.
8	Baseball.	17	Prism.
9	Phi Beta Kappa.	18	Kenny G.
10	*A Chorus Line*.	19	Bridget.
		20	West Point.

Round Fifty-Four

1 The theme song of what television show is "Tossed Salads and Scrambled Eggs?"

2 Step-Well insoles are trade-marked products of which 97-year-old foot care company?

3 In literature, which Brontë sister wrote the 1847 novel *Jane Eyre*: Emily or Charlotte?

4 From the French for "petticoat," what formal ball is held to introduce young women to society?

5 Who currently airs the show *In a Heartbeat*: Playboy Channel or Disney Channel?

6 In the video game *Super Mario Brothers*, what is the name of Mario's brother?

7 From sanskrit for "blowing out," what "N" is the Buddhist state of nothingness?

8 The movie *That Thing You Do!* was the first feature directed by which actor?

9 What novel, based on the 1992 U.S. Presidential campaign was published anonymously?

10 What children's modeling compound was developed by Rainbow Crafts and first sold in 1956?

11 Lindsay Buckingham wrote *Go Your Own Way*, during his break-up with which Fleetwood Mac singer?

12 Which member of the British Royal Family married Sophie Rhys-Jones in 1999?

13 In the 1970s, Harvey Milk was a U.S. politician and gay rights activist in what city?

14 In 2001, Kim Gandy replaced Patricia Ireland as president of what feminist group?

WEAKEST LINK

15 In the title of the Alexander Dumas tale, Athos, Porthos and Aramis were known collectively as what?

16 If a piece of music is marked *pianissimo*, is it intended to be played softly or loudly?

17 Which weekly news magazine published its first issue in February of 1933?

18 In television, what is the name of the strip club where mobster Tony Soprano keeps a back office?

19 In math, what is seven to the first power?

20 Which Australian actress from *Ally McBeal* appears in ads for L'Oreal shampoo?

Answers

1	*Frasier.*	12	Prince Edward (Earl of Wessex).
2	(Dr.) Scholl's.		
3	Charlotte.	13	San Francisco.
4	Cotillion (Cotillon)	14	N.O.W. (National Organization for Women).
5	Disney Channel.		
6	Luigi.		
7	Nirvana.	15	*The Three Musketeers.*
8	Tom Hanks.		
9	*Primary Colors.*	16	Softly.
10	Play-Doh.	17	*Newsweek.*
11	Stevie Nicks.	18	Bada Bing.
		19	Seven.
		20	Portia De Rossi.

Round Fifty-Five

1   In movies, who played Tom Ripley in *The Talented Mr. Ripley*?

2   What is the last name of the Dean Young comic-strip couple, Blondie and Dagwood?

3   Which radio talk show host and Watergate burglar wrote an autobiography entitled *Will*?

4   On which island in the South Atlantic did Napoleon Bonaparte spend his final days?

5   Before going solo, Ricky Martin was a member of what popular Latin boy band?

6   Which clay often used in architecture gets its name from the Italian for "Baked Earth?"

7   Which cellphone company headquartered in Stockholm, Sweden, started as a telegraph repair shop?

8   First published in 1953, what Ray Bradbury novel is set in a futuristic world where books are forbidden?

9   What long inner bone of the leg, located between the knee and the ankle, is also called the shinbone?

10   Which TV court show is presided over by a woman whose last name is Sheindlin?

11   In 1962, what artist became famous for his paintings of Campbell's soup cans?

12   What do the letters "MD" stand for when referring to the MD11 and MD80 commercial aircraft?

13   In movies, Kevin Costner won an Academy Award for directing what movie?

14   Which of the 13 colonies was founded by British clergyman Roger Williams?

15   What hotel owner known as "The Queen of Mean," served 18 months in prison for tax evasion?

16 Both Thomas Jefferson and John Adams died on which date in 1826?

17 In music, what stage name did Brian Warner create by combining a Hollywood sex symbol with a cult leader?

18 Danish architect Yorn Utzon designed what Australian building to resemble a giant sailing ship?

19 In theatre, what term for "actor" comes from the name of the poet who originated Greek tragedy?

20 In what movie did Jeff and Beau Bridges play musical brothers Jack and Frank?

125,000

75,000

50,000

25,000

10,000

5,000

2,500

1,000

BANKED

Answers

1	Matt Damon.	13	*Dances With Wolves.*
2	Bumstead.	14	Rhode Island.
3	G. Gordon Liddy.	15	Leona Helmsley.
4	St. Helena.	16	Independence Day (4 July).
5	Menudo.	17	Marilyn Manson.
6	Terracotta.	18	Sydney Opera House.
7	Ericsson.	19	Thespian.
8	*Fahrenheit 451.*	20	*The Fabulous Baker Boys.*
9	Tibia.		
10	*Judge Judy.*		
11	Andy Warhol.		
12	McDonnell Douglas.		

TOTAL

Round Fifty-Six

1 What current New York State capital is located on the Hudson River?

2 What Ray Anthony hit song inspired a line-dance during which people jump like rabbits?

3 Which U.S. muffler company shares its name with the mythical king that had the golden touch?

4 In music, what was the name of Elvis Presley's manager who went by the honorary title of Colonel?

5 The United Nations' International Court of Justice is located in what city?

6 Which American patriot is credited with the quote. "I only regret that I have but one life to lose for my country?"

7 Related to the llama, what "A" is a South American mammal that is prized for its wool?

8 Which cable channel airs the show *The F.B.I. Files*, and shares its name with a NASA Space Shuttle?

9 In Medicine, the hippo-campus is located within what organ of the human body?

10 What actress and screenwiter of *Sense and Sensibility* is the former wife of actor Kenneth Branagh?

11 Made of apples, celery and walnuts, what "W" is a salad named for a New York Park Avenue hotel?

12 British author Helen Fielding wrote a best-selling novel about the diary of what fictional character?

13 The initial Flag Act of the Continental Congress stated that how many stars would appear on the first American Flag?

14 What restaurant chain founded in Clearwater, Florida, in 1983 has an owl as its mascot?

WEAKEST LINK

15 In Music, R&B record producer Kenneth Edmonds is best known by what youthful nickname?

16 What brand of plastic storage bags introduced the "Gripper Zipper?"

17 In television, what former Congressman played Gopher on *The Love Boat*?

18 In astronomy, what is the closest star to the earth?

19 William Levitt's first mass-produced housing-community called Levittown is on what New York island?

20 In law, what do the letters in the traffic offense DUI stand for?

125,000

75,000

50,000

25,000

10,000

5,000

2,500

1,000

BANKED

TOTAL

Answers

1	Albany.	12	Bridget Jones.
2	Bunny Hop	13	Thirteen.
3	Midas.	14	Hooters (of America).
4	Tom Parker.		
5	The Hague (Den Haag/ Gravenhage).	15	Babyface.
		16	Ziploc (Storage Bags).
6	Nathan Hale.	17	Fred Grandy.
7	Alpaca.	18	The Sun.
8	Discovery.	19	Long Island.
9	Brain.	20	Driving (Under) the Influence.
10	Emma Thompson.		
11	Waldorf.		

Round Fifty-Seven

1 In religion, what is a book in the New Testament: Joel or Jude?

2 What magazine about decorating and landscaping is known by the initials BH&G?

3 In politics, by what common name is the handgun legislation named after President Reagan's former press secretary?

4 Magic the Dog and Morgan Fairchild have appeared in commercials for which clothing store chain?

5 In nature, what "K" is a variety of large brown seaweed common in North America and Japan?

6 Cargo pants and mini-skirts are part of the 2001 uniform of what 89 year-old organization?

7 They have now developed more than 950 flavors, but which national ice cream chain is known for their original 31?

8 In music, what Shannon Hoon band featured the "Bee Girl" in the video for its single "No Rain?"

9 In a 1980 re-match against Sugar Ray Leonard, what boxer quit, proclaiming "No Mas" ("No More") in the eighth round?

10 In science, what "H" is the branch of zoology that deals strictly with reptiles and amphibians?

11 On what game show, hosted by Peter Tomarken, would contestants lose all their money if they got a "Whammy"?

12 In literature, what Charles Dickens novel features the character Uriah Heep?

13 Which network equipment company briefly surpassed Microsoft in March 2000 for the world's highest market cap?

14 What movie, featuring Halle Berry and Don Cheadle, deals with the world of computer hackers?

15 What does the letter "C" stand for in the birthing method known as a "C-Section?"

WEAKEST LINK

16 Destroyed by the Romans, the ancient city of Carthage was located on what continent?

17 Also known as King Charles I, who did Pope Leo III crown as the first Holy Roman Emperor?

18 In theater, what actor wrote and performed the monologue show *Swimming To Cambodia*?

19 In television, what New Zealand-born actress played Xena in *Xena: Warrior Princess*?

20 In finance, what Berkshire Hathaway chairman is known as "The Oracle of Omaha?"

Answers

1	Jude.	12	*David Copperfield.*
2	*Better Homes & Gardens.*	13	Cisco (Systems).
3	The Brady Bill.	14	*Swordfish.*
4	Old Navy.	15	Caesarean.
5	Kelp.	16	Africa.
6	Girl Scouts of America (GSA).	17	Charlemagne (Charles the Great).
7	Baskin-Robbins.		
8	Blind Melon.	18	Spalding Gray.
9	Roberto Duran.	19	Lucy Lawless.
10	Herpetology.	20	Warren Buffett.
11	*Press Your Luck.*		

Round Fifty-Eight

1 In Tantric Buddhism, the psychic energy-centers of the body are referred to by which Sanskrit word for "wheel?"

2 Which HBO talk show host wrote the book *I Rant Therefore I Am*?

3 In terms of acreage grown, what is the leading crop in the U.S.?

4 What French lawn game is played by the Queen of Hearts in *Alice's Adventures in Wonderland*?

5 In which 1984 movie did Arnold Schwarzenegger first deliver the tag-line "I'll be back?"

6 What adult magazine was founded by Bob Guccione in 1965?

7 What was the first widely-used brand of disposable diaper introduced by Procter & Gamble?

8 Denny Laine and Joe English were members of what Paul McCartney band?

9 In 1981, who shot President Reagan?

10 What is one P.M. in U.S. military time?

11 Which process is used to produce beer: distillation or fermentation?

12 In geography, the city of Milwaukee, Wisconsin, is located on which of the Great Lakes?

13 In business, which Pennsylvania company manufactures Chocolate Kisses?

14 In movies, which actress played young Rose in the film *Titanic*?

15 In literature, which author and humanitarian wrote *The Good Earth*?

16 In cartoons, Jay Ward's animated character Rocky was what kind of flying rodent?

17 What is the highest star rating bestowed by the *Mobil Travel Guide to Restaurants and Hotels*?

18 In music, which singer has won Grammys for "Sweet Child O' Mine" and "All I Wanna Do?"

19 Who was the first African-American mayor of Los Angeles?

20 In 1981, actress Carol Burnett won a libel lawsuit against what tabloid?

Answers

1	Chakra.	13	Hershey's
2	Dennis Miller.	14	Kate Winslet.
3	Corn.	15	Pearl Buck.
4	Croquet.	16	Squirrel.
5	*The Terminator*.	17	Five.
6	*Penthouse*.	18	Sheryl Crow.
7	Pampers.	19	Tom Bradley.
8	(Paul McCartney and) Wings.	20	*National Enquirer*.
9	John Hinckley (Jr).		
10	1300 hours.		
11	Fermentation.		
12	Michigan.		

PREVIOUS TOTAL

125,000

75,000

50,000

25,000

10,000

5,000

2,500

1,000

BANKED

TOTAL

Round Fifty-Nine

1 In television, the Flintstones were residents of which prehistoric town?

2 In astronomy, which planet is larger in diameter: Earth or Neptune?

3 In the New Testament, how many pieces of silver was Judas paid to betray Jesus?

4 In radio, what Cleveland disc jockey coined the term "rock and roll?"

5 Oscar-winning actress Geena Davis took part in the U.S. trials to compete in the 2000 Olympic Games in what sport?

6 In music, the backup band for Buddy Holly shared its name with what insects?

7 What actress from *White Men Can't Jump* started her career as a dancer on *Soul Train*?

8 Which is the only Ivy League university located in New Jersey?

9 In medicine, the name of which psychological disorder is derived from the Greek words for "Spider" and "Fear?"

10 In literature, which author read her poem "On the Pulse of Morning" at President Clinton's first Inauguration?

11 In movies, which actor won an Oscar for his performance as Christie Brown in *My Left Foot*?

12 Which monarch was the most recent King of England: George VI or Edward VIII?

13 Which public opinion polling organization was founded by a Northwestern University journalism professor?

14 In music, who is the lead singer of The Miami Sound Machine?

15 In 1969, what ukulele-playing singer married Miss Vicki on *The Tonight Show*?

16 In geography, what river runs from Colorado to the Gulf of Mexico, and forms the border between Mexico and Texas?

17 Timothy Daly and David Janssen both played Dr. Richard Kimble in different versions of which T.V. series?

18 In anatomy, which triangular muscle covering the shoulder joint is used to raise the arm from the side?

19 Named for an Al Capp comic strip character, on which holiday do women ask men to dances?

20 What "H" is the scientific name for growing plants. In a water nutrient solution rather than in soil?

Answers

1 Bedrock.
2 Neptune.
3 Thirty.
4 Alan Freed.
5 Archery.
6 Crickets.
7 Rosie Perez.
8 Princeton.
9 Arachnaphobia.
10 Maya Angelou.
11 Daniel Day-Lewis.
12 George VI.
13 Gallup.
14 Gloria Estefan.
15 Tiny Tim.
16 Rio Grande (Bravo).
17 *The Fugitive*.
18 Deltoid (Delt).
19 Sadie Hawkins Day.
20 Hydroponics.

PREVIOUS TOTAL

125,000

75,000

50,000

25,000

10,000

5,000

2,500

1,000

BANKED

TOTAL

Round Sixty

1 In movies, Michael Clarke Duncan received an Oscar nomination for which Stephen King film?

2 Who was the President of the U.S. during World War I?

3 In pop music, which band went platinum with their CD *Enema of the State?*

4 Which Teenage Mutant Ninja Turtle is named for the Florentine sculptor of "The Feast of Herod?"

5 In math, what is five squared?

6 Which former host of *It's Showtime at the Apollo*, currently stars in his own self-titled sitcom?

7 In botany, what is the pollen-producing male organ of a flower called?

8 In geography, the Americas were named after which Italian explorer?

9 Before he became mayor of New York, Rudy Giuliani held which office whose title is abbreviated D.A.?

10 Which nation did the U.N. support during the Korean War: North Korea or South Korea?

11 In classical music, *Fidelio* was the only opera written by what German composer?

12 Jean de Brunhoff wrote several stories featuring which elephant who became king of the forest?

13 In history, Fidel Castro came to power in Cuba after which dictator fled the country?

14 What popular name was given to the seniors' organization founded by Maggie Coon to address the problems faced by retirees?

15 In which Fox night-time soap-opera did characters frequent a bar called Shooters?

WEAKEST LINK

16 In medicine, what "T" is the clinical name for the infectious disease also called lockjaw?

17 Counter-balance, counter-march, and jack are types of what machine used for weaving cloth?

18 Which U.S. city is home to the Will Rogers World Airport?

19 Which film critic wrote the screenplay for the movie *Beyond the Valley of the Dolls*?

20 Indicted for war crimes in 1999, who was the president of the Federal Republic of Yugoslavia from 1997 to 2000?

125,000

75,000

50,000

25,000

10,000

5,000

2,500

1,000

BANKED

Answers

1	*The Green Mile.*	11	Ludwig van Beethoven.
2	Woodrow Wilson.	12	Babar.
3	Blink 182.	13	(Fulgencio) Batista.
4	Donatello.	14	Gray Panthers.
5	Twenty-five.	15	*Melrose Place.*
6	Steve Harvey.	16	Tetanus (Trismus).
7	Stamen.	17	Loom.
8	Amerigo Vespucci.	18	Oklahoma City.
9	District Attorney.	19	Roger Ebert.
10	South Korea.	20	Slobodan Milosevic.

TOTAL

Round Sixty-One

1 In soccer, which nation hosted and won the 1998 men's World Cup?

2 A.N.C. is an abbreviation for which political organization once headed by Nelson Mandela?

3 What oily, explosive liquid is used to make both dynamite and heart medicine?

4 Which TV news anchor wrote the book *The Greatest Generation*?

5 In the animal kingdom, the males of which equine fish carry eggs in a pouch on their stomachs?

6 In literature, the heroic Hazel attempts to lead his fellow rabbits to safety in which 1972 Richard Adams novel?

7 What rotary engine that produces electricity gets its name from the Latin for "whirl?"

8 In movies, who directed the classic 1939 Western *Stagecoach*?

9 In transportation, Varig is the national airline of which South American country?

10 Which type of animal is a gazelle: deer or antelope?

11 In geography, what is the southernmost country of the Balkan Peninsula?

12 In folk music, what Harvard-Square street-performer had a top ten hit with the song "Fast Car?"

13 Which company introduced cranberry juice cocktail in 1930?

14 Which actor sent a woman called Sacheen Little-Feather to refuse his 1973 Academy Award?

15 What street in Monterey, California, is named after a John Steinbeck novel?

WEAKEST LINK

16 Which medical procedure uses a transducer probe to allow doctors to view an unborn child?

17 Which best-selling romance author wrote *Lady Boss* and *Hollywood Wives*?

18 Which U.S. President's program of national reform was known as The Great Society?

19 In fashion, what necktie knot was named for an English duke who abdicated his throne for Wallis Simpson?

20 David Letterman attended what Indiana university?

Answers

1	France.	13	Ocean Spray.
2	African National Congress.	14	Marlon Brando.
		15	Cannery Row.
3	Nitro-glycerine.	16	Ultrasound (Sonograph).
4	Tom Brokaw.		
5	Sea-horse (Pipefish).	17	Jackie Collins.
6	*Watership Down*.	18	Lyndon (Baines) Johnson.
7	Turbine.		
8	John Ford.	19	(Half) Windsor.
9	Brazil.	20	Ball State.
10	Antelope.		
11	Greece.		
12	Tracy Chapman.		

PREVIOUS TOTAL

125,000

75,000

50,000

25,000

10,000

5,000

2,500

1,000

BANKED

TOTAL

Round Sixty-Two

1 What "R" is a wooden musical wind instrument of the flute family?

2 What annual East Coast Race, first held in 1970, currently begins in Staten Island and ends at Tavern on the Green?

3 In astronomy, what American physicist first discovered the belts of radiation that circle the Earth?

4 The jungle known as the Darien Gap is shared by Colombia and which Central American nation?

5 In television, what Minnesota Vikings quarterback co-hosted *That's Incredible*?

6 Which of the following foods contain cholesterol: Peanuts or Salmon?

7 Which Milton Bradley "Capture-the-flag" board game features Spies, Scouts and Bombs?

8 In math, what is thirty-seven multiplied by three?

9 In which 1955 movie does Marilyn Monroe stand over a subway grate as the wind blows her dress up?

10 In literature, who wrote the novels *The Loved One* and *Brideshead Revisited*?

11 In medicine, which drug is classified as an anti-depressant: Zantac or Zoloft?

12 Which French author wrote a *Dictionary of Philosophy* as well as the novel *Candide*?

13 What "G" were the nomadic horsemen of the Argentine Pampas in the early 19th century?

14 What Russian word, meaning "openness," was a policy initiated by Mikhail Gorbachev in the 1980s?

15 In baseball, what does the acronym E.R.A. stand for?

WEAKEST LINK

16 What "K" is the carved wooden doll representing the invisible spirits of the Pueblo Indian tribes?

17 Which scientist has an element named after him: Niels Bohr or William Nye?

18 In music, what Australian singer opened a chain of clothing stores called Koala Blue?

19 In 1979, Black & Decker introduced the first cordless vacuum cleaner known by what name?

20 Which actor is married to Catherine Zeta Jones?

Answers

1	Recorder.	11	Zoloft.
2	New York City Marathon.	12	Voltaire.
		13	Gaucho(s).
3	(James Alfred) Van Allen.	14	Glasnost.
4	Panama.	15	Earned Run Average.
5	Fran Tarkenton.	16	Kachina (Kachinam).
6	Salmon		
7	(Ultimate) Stratego.	17	Niels Bohr.
8	111.	18	Olivia Newton-John.
9	*The Seven-Year Itch.*	19	Dustbuster.
10	Evelyn Waugh.	20	Michael Douglas.

PREVIOUS TOTAL

125,000

75,000

50,000

25,000

10,000

5,000

2,500

1,000

BANKED

TOTAL

Round Sixty-Three

1 Until 1990, Checkpoint Charlie was the crossing point between the East and West parts of which European city?

2 What Gene Hackman movie is about a cruise ship turned upside-down by a tidal wave?

3 In fashion, what "M" is the long silky hair from the fleece of an angora goat?

4 The Constitution specifically states that the time between one U.S. Census and the next cannot exceed how many years?

5 In food, what shellfish is traditionally featured in the French dish, Coquilles St. Jacques?

6 In Television, Agent Cooper ate cherry pie at the Double R. Diner in which David Lynch series?

7 In ads for the National Federation of Coffee Growers of Colombia, Juan Valdez stands next to what animal?

8 In literature, which American novelist created Tarzan of the Apes?

9 In history, which British Prime Minister signed the 1938 Munich Pact with Hitler?

10 In music, "Stand by Your Man" was originally recorded by which country artist?

11 Which branch of mathematics, studying continuously changing values, was co-created by Isaac Newton?

12 Which American city is home to the 630 foot-tall Gateway Arch?

13 In science, which bitter alkaloid is a stimulant found in coffee, tea, and kola nuts?

14 In medicine, malaria is caused by the bite of what species of insect?

15 In music, Walter Becker and Donald Fagen are better known by what band name?

16 In Geography, the cities of Salzburg and Vienna are both located in what European country?

17 Which talk show had a longer run: *The Chevy Chase Show* or *The Magic Hour*?

18 In astronomy, from the Latin word for "new," what "N" is an exploding star?

19 The Chunnel connects Great Britain and what other European country?

20 What female star of Buffalo Bill's Wild West Show was billed as "Little Sure-Shot?"

Answers

1	Berlin.	11	Calculus.
2	*The Poseidon Adventure.*	12	St. Louis (Missouri).
3	Mohair.	13	Caffeine.
4	Ten years.	14	(Anopheline) mosquitos
5	Scallops.	15	Steely Dan.
6	*Twin Peaks.*	16	Austria.
7	Mule.	17	*The Magic Hour.*
8	Edgar Rice Burroughs.	18	Nova.
9	Neville Chamberlain.	19	France.
10	Tammy Wynette.	20	Annie Oakley.

PREVIOUS TOTAL

125,000

75,000

50,000

25,000

10,000

5,000

2,500

1,000

BANKED

TOTAL

Round Sixty-Four

1 Located in the Badger State, what university's mascot is Bucky Badger?

2 In movies, who directed the Ben Affleck film *Pearl Harbor*?

3 What hotel chain founder authored the book *Be My Guest*?

4 Hugh Lofting wrote a series of books featuring what character who talked to the animals?

5 In history, which U.S. State did not secede during the Civil War: Arkansas or Kentucky?

6 In fashion, which knee-length men's skirt is worn by Scottish regiments in the British army?

7 What comic-strip detective, created by Chester Gould, married Tess Trueheart?

8 In food, what chicken dish is named after the capital of Ukraine?

9 In television, which Fox animated show features a Texas propane salesman?

10 Which U.S. holiday is named for the patron saint of lovers?

11 What country music artist inspired a dance craze, with his hit song "Achy Breaky Heart?"

12 In what movie did Faye Dunaway play Joan Crawford?

13 In games, what is the No. 1 selling brand of playing cards in the U.S.?

14 In law, what "J" is the group of twelve people chosen to give a verdict on a case?

15 In television, what actress played Mallory Keaton on the series *Family Ties*?

16 Created by cartoonist Johnny Gruelle, what cloth doll had red hair and a brother named Andy?

WEAKEST LINK

17 What former Miss America was the first female sportscaster on *The N.F.L. Today*?

18 What celebrity was the main subject of the Bob Woodward book *Wired*?

19 In medicine, what is the largest artery in the human body?

20 What Bruce Springsteen album includes the songs "Thunder Road" and "Jungleland?"

125,000

75,000

50,000

25,000

10,000

5,000

2,500

1,000

BANKED

Answers

1	University of Wisconsin.	11	Billy Ray Cyrus.
2	Michael Bay.	12	*Mommie Dearest*.
3	Conrad (Nicholson) Hilton.	13	Bicycle.
4	*Doctor Dolittle*.	14	Jury.
5	Kentucky.	15	Justine Bateman.
6	Kilt.	16	Raggedy Ann.
7	Dick Tracy.	17	Phyllis George (Linda Banks).
8	(Chicken) Kiev.	18	John Belushi.
9	*King of the Hill*.	19	Aorta.
10	St. Valentine's Day.	20	*Born To Run*.

TOTAL

Round Sixty-Five

1   In math, what is one thousand divided by one hundred?

2   In Language, which one of Aristotle's four elements is referred to by the Greek prefix "pyro?"

3   In what movie does James Caan play a writer held prisoner by a deranged fan?

4   In geography, Bismarck is the capital city of what U.S. State?

5   What *Arabian Nights* folk hero discovered the hidden gold of the forty thieves?

6   Billy Crystal, Robin Williams, and Whoopi Goldberg were the first hosts of which H.B.O. comedy telethon for the homeless?

7   Which treaty between the U.S. and England formally ended the American Revolution?

8   What early incarnation of the movie theatre was so named because the cost of admission was five cents?

9   The Petrified Forest and the Painted Desert are both features of which U.S. State?

10 In music, which rock band recorded the albums *Dark Side of the Moon* and *The Wall*?

11 After it was installed in a Houston baseball park, "Chem-grass" was changed to what trademarked name?

12 In history, "Tania" was the alias of what kidnapped newspaper heiress?

13 In television, what actor starred in the title roles *Perry Mason* and *Ironside*?

14 What housewife and mother wrote the nationally syndicated humor column, "At Wit's End?"

15 What sport is the central subject of the movie *Tin Cup*?

16 In politics, what female former governor of Texas lost her bid for re-election to George W. Bush?

17 *Pride and Prejudice* is a novel by which English author born in 1775?

18 What is the most populous city in Portugal?

19 In television, what was the name of the Cartwright's ranch on the western *Bonanza*?

20 The wives of the first and third U.S. Presidents shared what first name?

PREVIOUS TOTAL

125,000

75,000

50,000

25,000

10,000

5,000

2,500

1,000

BANKED

TOTAL

Answers

1	Ten.	14	Erma Bombeck.
2	Fire.	15	Golf.
3	*Misery*.	16	Ann Richards.
4	North Dakota.	17	Jane Austen.
5	Ali Baba.	18	Lisbon (Lisboa).
6	Comic Relief.	19	Ponderosa.
7	Treaty of Paris.	20	Martha.
8	Nickelodeon.		
9	Arizona.		
10	Pink Floyd.		
11	Astroturf.		
12	Patty (Patricia) Hearst.		
13	Raymond Burr.		

Round Sixty-Six

1   In business, which car rental company uses the slogan, "We try harder?"

2   What "S" is the mountain-dwelling people of Nepal who have gained recognition as porters in the Himalaya mountain range?

3   What married pop duo won a Grammy for "Love Will Keep Us Together?"

4   What programming language developed by Sun Microsystems, shares its name with a type of coffee?

5   In *Alice in Wonderland*, what character would vanish but leave behind its beaming grin?

6   In medicine, the name of what tightly-wound bandage comes from the French word for "turn"?

7   In movies, what actress played a prostitute as the female lead in *Leaving Las Vegas*?

8   What tree-dwelling marsupial, named Vic, Is featured in advertisements for Quantas Airlines?

9   From the Greek for "single speech," what is the dramatic soliloquy delivered by a character in a play?

10 Before playing a detective on *N.Y.P.D. Blue*, Jimmy Smits played an attorney on which television series?

11 What is the English language name for the inland sea bounded by Turkey on the south and Russia on the north and east?

12 In music, what New York punk-band originally released the song "I Wanna Be Sedated?"

13 What unit of sound measurement derives its name from the inventor of the telephone?

14 In art, which frequent contributor to *Playboy* magazine, has also been the official artist of Five Olympiads?

15 In movies, who co-wrote and directed the film *Young Frankenstein?*

16 Which Margaret Wise-Brown book features a little rabbit and a "quiet old lady whispering hush?"

17 Which star of the series *My Sister Sam* is married to actor Mark Harmon?

18 The world's smallest flying mammal is the hog-nosed variety of what animal?

19 What news program began in 1979 as a nightly report, called *The Iran Crisis: America Held Hostage?*

20 Where in California would you find the main campus of Pepperdine University?

PREVIOUS TOTAL

125,000

75,000

50,000

25,000

10,000

5,000

2,500

1,000

BANKED

TOTAL

Answers

1	Avis.	14	Leroy Niemann.
2	Sherpa.	15	Mel Brooks.
3	Captain And Tennille.	16	*Goodnight Moon.*
4	Java.	17	Pam Dawber.
5	Cheshire Cat.	18	Bat.
6	Tourniquet.	19	*Nightline.*
7	Elizabeth Shue.	20	Malibu.
8	Koala (bear).		
9	Monologue.		
10	*L.A. Law.*		
11	Black Sea.		
12	The Ramones.		
13	Decibel (scale).		

Round Sixty-Seven

1 What pest control service, founded in 1901, sponsors an insect zoo at the National Museum of Natural History?

2 The affliction known as gingivitis is characterized by an inflammation of what part of the mouth?

3 What beat-driven 1970s dance style derived its name from the French word for "record library?"

4 Along with Belize, what country borders Mexico on the south?

5 What English monarch broke with the Roman Catholic church over his divorce from Catherine of Aragon?

6 What rap-duo starred in the three *House Party* movies?

7 In math, what is three multiplied by two, multiplied by one, multiplied by zero?

8 In fashion, which Italian designer label, known for its handbags, uses a double "F" logo?

9 What Louisiana city has hosted the annual Jazz and Heritage Festival for more than 25 years?

10 In the game of craps, what number is statistically most likely to be rolled?

11 In television, what former attorney created the series *Picket Fences* and *The Practice*?

12 What talking doll, introduced in 1960, said "I'm hungry," and "Will you play with me?"

13 In food, which popular dip takes its name from the Arabic word for "chickpea?"

14 In music, what soul singer recorded the hit "Midnight Train to Georgia," with her backing singers "The Pips"?

15 Which Nabisco cookie was invented by Charles Roser and named for a New England town?

WEAKEST LINK

16 What country has won the most Nobel Prizes in Physics?

17 In geography, which U.S. state capital city is located on the Delaware River?

18 In what film do nerds Gary and Wyatt create a woman with their computer?

19 Before becoming president, Franklin D. Roosevelt was elected to which New York State office in 1928?

20 The state flag of Rhode Island features thirteen Stars encircling what nautical device?

Answers

1	Orkin.	14	Gladys Knight.
2	Gums.	15	(Fig) Newton.
3	Disco (Discotheque).	16	United States.
4	Guatemala.	17	Trenton (New Jersey).
5	King Henry VIII.	18	*Weird Science*.
6	Kid 'N Play.	19	Governor.
7	Zero.	20	(Golden ship's) Anchor.
8	Fendi.		
9	New Orleans.		
10	Seven.		
11	David E. Kelley.		
12	Chatty Cathy.		
13	Humous.		

Round Sixty-Eight

1   In the World War II Battle Of Midway, U.S. bombers sunk four aircraft-carriers of which nation?

2   Before joining the Lakers, who coached the Chicago Bulls to six N.B.A. Championships?

3   What 1980s girl group, fronted by singer Belinda Carlisle, had a hit with "Our Lips Are Sealed?"

4   What U.S.D.A. Forest Service mascot teaches children: "Only YOU can prevent forest fires?"

5   What title is given to the Chief Executive of the United Nations?

6   What is the name of the used-car price-publication, first started by Les Kelley?

7   Known as the "Great Stone Face," which silent film-comedian directed and starred in *The General*?

8   What "R" is the brand of toothpaste that shares its name with a 17th-century Dutch painter?

9   Located on the island of New Providence, what city is the capital of the Bahamas?

10   In television, what actor played characters named Tony on both *Taxi* and *Who's the Boss*?

11   Martin Luther King's 1963 "I Have a Dream" speech was given on the steps of what National Monument?

12   Howie Long and Teri Hatcher appear in commercials for which electronics store?

13   In the Old Testament, God gave the Ten Commandments to which prophet?

14   In music, which guitar legend is married to actress Valerie Bertinelli?

WEAKEST LINK

125,000

75,000

50,000

25,000

10,000

5,000

2,500

1,000

15 Bell Atlantic and G.T.E. merged to form which new communications company?

16 From the Latin for "wise man," to which species do modern humans belong?

17 Which actor portrayed troubled teen Jim Stark in the film *Rebel Without a Cause*?

18 What kitchen appliance is also the nickname given to ex-Chicago Bear football player William Perry?

19 What Broadway Composer wrote the music and lyrics for *A Little Night Music*?

20 Which Chevrolet car was the subject of Ralph Nader's book, *Unsafe At Any Speed*?

Answers

1	Japan.	11	Lincoln Memorial.
2	Phil Jackson.	12	Radio Shack.
3	The Go-Gos.	13	Moses (Moshe)
4	Smokey (the) Bear.	14	Eddie Van Halen.
5	Secretary General.	15	Verizon.
6	(Kelley) Blue Book (of Motor Car Values).	16	Homo Sapiens.
		17	James Dean.
7	Buster Keaton.	18	Refrigerator (The Fridge).
8	Rembrandt.	19	Stephen Sondheim.
9	Nassau.	20	Corvair.
10	Tony Danza.		

BANKED

TOTAL

Round Sixty-Nine

1 In geography, Ulan Bator is the capital city of which country?

2 The athlete Jesse Owens won his first Olympic Games gold medal in what city?

3 In pop, Mick Jagger is the lead singer of which British music group?

4 In movies, what actor traveled through time in the film *Back to the Future*?

5 In TV's *The Simpsons*, what is the name of the Mayor of Springfield?

6 What does the acronym NATO stand for?

7 The Berlin Wall fell in which decade: 1980s or 1990s?

8 In education, an Associate's Degree is typically earned in how many years?

9 The Dow Jones Industrial Average is primarily made up of stocks from what exchange?

10 Until his retirement in 2001, Jack Welch was the CEO of what major American conglomerate?

11 In poetry, traditionally, how many lines are there in a sonnet?

12 How many ounces are there in the US measure of one pint?

13 In anatomy, what part of the body does a nephrologist treat?

14 How many engines are there on a Boeing 747 Jumbo Jet aircraft?

15 In geography, which U.S. state is on the other side Nebraska's northern border?

16 In math, a compass, or pair of compasses, is a tool used to do what?

WEAKEST LINK

17 In literature, which survivor of the Nazi Holocaust wrote *Night*?

18 In the animal kingdom, which can exist longer without water: a camel or a rat?

19 What the only national monuments in the U.S. that are mobile?

20 Who is the patron saint of Scotland?

PREVIOUS TOTAL

125,000

75,000

50,000

25,000

10,000

5,000

2,500

1,000

BANKED

TOTAL

Answers

1	Mongolia.	11	Fourteen.
2	Berlin.	12	Sixteen.
3	The Rolling Stones.	13	Kidneys.
4	Michael J. Fox.	14	Four.
5	Mayor Quimby.	15	South Dakota.
6	North Atlantic Treaty Organization.	16	Draw circles.
7	1980s.	17	Elie Wiesel.
8	Two.	18	A rat.
9	New York Stock Exchange.	19	San Francisco cable cars.
10	General Electric.	20	St. Andrew.

Round Seventy

1 In religion, which man was the first Pope?

2 What "P" is the smallest primate on earth?

3 A fedora is an item of clothing, but is it a type of shoe or a type of hat?

4 Australia was originally started as what type of colony for Britain?

5 In science, what is the chemical symbol for water.

6 Where is the headquarters of the retail corporation Walmart?

7 *The Cherry Orchard* and *The Three Sisters* were both written by which Russian playwright?

8 In geography, of which country is the city of Paramaribo the capital.

9 What was the last year the Boston Red Sox won baseball's World Series?

10 In music, which artist recorded the multi-million-selling album *Born to Run*?

11 The Hoosiers is the nickname of which university's sports teams?

12 Who played Hawkeye Pierce in the movie version of *M*A*S*H*?

13 What is the current name for the Asian country formerly known as Burma?

14 What is the name of the salesman in Arthur Miller's play *Death of a Salesman*?

15 In history, which U.S. president liked Fresca soda so much, he had a tap installed in the White House?

16 In anatomy, what is the common name for the tympanic membrane?

WEAKEST LINK

17 Born in 1694 which French writer was the author of *Candide*?

18 On which television sitcom would you find siblings Ross and Monica Geller?

19 How many feet are there in one mile?

20 In what U.S. state is the brick-by-brick reconstruction of London Bridge located?

PREVIOUS TOTAL

125,000

75,000

50,000

25,000

10,000

5,000

2,500

1,000

BANKED

TOTAL

Answers

1	(The Apostle) Peter.	11	Indiana University.
2	Pygmy marmoset.	12	Donald Sutherland.
3	Hat.	13	Myanmar
4	Prison (Penal).	14	Willie Loman.
5	H_2O.	15	Lyndon (Baines) Johnson.
6	Arkansas.	16	The eardrum.
7	Anton Chekhov.	17	Voltaire (François Marie Aronet).
8	Surinam	18	*Friends*.
9	1918.	19	5,280.
10	Bruce Springsteen.	20	Arizona.

Round Seventy-One

1 Which hallucinogenic drug was developed by Dr. Albert Hofmann and became popular during the 1960's hippie movement?

2 Which Italian dictator was known as *il Duce*?

3 Which Welsh actor did Elizabeth Taylor marry and divorce twice?

4 Which country is closer to the borders of the United States: Russia or Bermuda?

5 What "M" is the French national anthem?

6 What was the real name of legendary baseball player Babe Ruth?

7 In jazz, Miles Davis is normally associated with playing which instrument?

8 Which television series featured a sheriff by the name of Rosco P. Coltrane?

9 Who seized the power from Nikita Khrushchev in 1964 to become leader of the Soviet Union?

10 In geography, what mountain range is home to Mount Holyoke, Amherst and Williams?

11 What is the full name of the food manufacturer contracted to "Nabisco?"

12 In which Italian city is the La Scala opera house located?

13 The musical *Godspell* was based on the gospel of which apostle?

14 In math, how many millimeters are there in a centimeter?

15 In movies, who directed the first film in *The Godfather* trilogy?

16 In science, what is the chemical symbol for carbon?

WEAKEST LINK

17 The United Nations Headquarters building is located in which city?

18 Which soldier and political leader of the 18th and 19th centuries is pictured on the US $10 bill?

19 Who is credited with inventing the sport of basketball?

20 What comic book caped crusader was created by Bob Kane?

PREVIOUS TOTAL

125,000

75,000

50,000

25,000

10,000

5,000

2,500

1,000

BANKED

TOTAL

Answers

1	LSD (lysergic acid diethylamide).	11	National Biscuit Company.
2	(Benito) Mussolini.	12	Milan.
3	Richard Burton.	13	St. Matthew.
4	Russia.	14	Ten.
5	Marseillaise.	15	Francis Ford Coppola.
6	George Herman Ruth.	16	C.
7	Trumpet.	17	New York City.
8	*The Dukes of Hazzard*.	18	Alexander Hamilton.
9	Leonid Brezhnev.	19	(Dr.) James Naismith.
10	The Berkshires.	20	Batman.

Round Seventy-Two

1 In science, what is the only rock that is regularly consumed by humans?

2 The Spanish author Miguel de Cervantes wrote which book that was later turned into the musical *Man of La Mancha*?

3 Penguins are found where the arctic or the antarctic?

4 In 1836, which U.S. state became the first home for a Mormon temple?

5 In math, (negative) 7 multiplied by (negative) 6 equals what?

6 In politics, the "Tea Pot Dome Scandal" happened during whose presidency?

7 In motoring, if an automobile is a coupé, how many doors does it have?

8 Which artist was born first: Vincent Van Gogh or Claude Monet?

9 In TV, the US cable network ESPN primarily shows what type of programming?

10 In the stock market, if you want to "short" a stock, are you hoping the price goes up or down?

11 Which play by William Shakespeare inspired the Broadway musical *Kiss Me Kate*?

12 In education, how long does it typically take to earn a Bachelor's degree.

13 Canadian Prime Minister Jean Chrétien hails from which province?

14 According to the title, in what century did the Buck Rodgers television series take place?

15 In music, Eubie Blake was famous for playing which instrument?

16 In sport, Vince Lombardi coached which NFL team to multiple championships?

17 What is the official language of the African country of Angola?

18 Which North American city has a larger population: Detroit or Cleveland?

19 In movies, the Oliver Stone film *Platoon* is set during which war?

20 The name of what group of extinct creatures comes from the Latin for "monstrous lizard?"

125,000

75,000

50,000

25,000

10,000

5,000

2,500

1,000

BANKED

TOTAL

Answers

1	Salt.	13	Quebec.
2	*Don Quixote.*	14	25th (century).
3	Antarctic.	15	Piano.
4	Ohio.	16	Green Bay Packers.
5	42.		
6	Warren G. Harding.	17	Portuguese.
7	Two.	18	Detroit.
8	Monet.	19	Vietnam War.
9	Sports.	20	Dinosaurs.
10	Down.		
11	*The Taming of the Shrew.*		
12	Four years.		

Round Seventy-Three

1 Which of the following schools is not in the Ivy League: Cornell, Amherst or Dartmouth?

2 The "West Bank" refers to the West Bank of which river in Israel?

3 Which sportsman referred to himself as "the luckiest man on the face of the earth" upon his retirement?

4 In music, which Crosby Stills and Nash song was written as a response to the murders at Kent State University in the 1960s?

5 In movies, who directed the first film in the *Star Wars* series?

6 Who was the President of South Africa prior to Nelson Mandela?

7 In business, what US state is home to the three major US automakers?

8 Which playwright was born first: William Shakespeare or Molière?

9 In which Washington D.C. theater was President Abraham Lincoln shot in 1865?

10 Which of the following wind instruments is not played using a reed – clarinet, flute or saxophone?

11 On the TV series *M*A*S*H*, Corporal Klinger hailed from what Midwestern city, home of baseball's Mud Hens?

12 What was the only state won by Walter Mondale in the 1984 Presidential election?

13 Aer Lingus is the national airline for what country?

14 In music, which singer's range is higher an alto or a tenor?

15 If someone is part of the Hudson River School are they a painter or a dancer?

16 In physics, force equals mass times what?

17 Which planet is closer to the Sun: Saturn or Uranus?

18 In games, how many playing cards are there in a standard deck?

19 What was the final job of economist Adam Smith?

20 In sport, the NBA basketball's Utah Jazz used to play in which city?

PREVIOUS TOTAL

125,000

75,000

50,000

25,000

10,000

5,000

2,500

1,000

BANKED

TOTAL

Answers

1	Amherst.	14	Alto.
2	River Jordan.	15	Painter.
3	Lou Gehrig.	16	Acceleration.
4	"Ohio."	17	Saturn.
5	George Lucas.	18	Fifty-two.
6	F.W. DeKlerk.	19	Customs official.
7	Michigan.	20	New Orleans.
8	Shakespeare.		
9	Ford's (Theater).		
10	Flute.		
11	Toledo (Ohio).		
12	Minnesota.		
13	Ireland		

Round Seventy-Four

1   In science, "Cl" is the chemical symbol for what substance?

2   In which American city would you find the building known as "Old Ironsides?"

3   What Rhode Island-based college is known by the acronym "RISD?"

4   In history, "Seward's Foley" was the name given to the U.S. purchase of what future state?

5   "Sugar Ray" Leonard had the same nickname as which boxing great?

6   Which state's university is sometimes called "U-Dub?"

7   "Who Shot J.R." was a cliffhanger episode for what night-time drama series and one the most-watched programs in television history?

8   A Moslem of mixed Arab and Berber decent living in North Africa is know as what?

9   In math, the shape called a quadrilateral is any figure with how many sides?

10 According to the ancient Greeks, what human organ was the center of the thought process?

11 Aeroflot is the national airline for what country?

12 The capital city of which African country is Algiers?

13 Conquest, Slaughter and Famine are three of the Four Horseman of the Apocalypse, who is the fourth?

14 Archie Bunker was the leading character in what long-running television comedy series?

15 In science, at what temperature on the Fahrenheit scale does water boil?

WEAKEST LINK

16 In music, Bill Monroe is recognized as the inventor of which type of music?

17 *Black Boy* was the title of a book written by which African-American author?

18 Buick cars are part of which American car company?

19 With which style of poetry were Byron and Tennyson both associated?

20 For which 1992 western did Clint Eastwood win the Oscar for Best Director?

PREVIOUS TOTAL

125,000

75,000

50,000

25,000

10,000

5,000

2,500

1,000

BANKED

Answers

1	Chlorine.	11	Russia.
2	Boston	12	Algeria.
3	Rhode Island School of Design.	13	Death.
		14	*All in the Family*.
		15	212° (degrees).
4	Alaska	16	Bluegrass.
5	Sugar Ray Robinson.	17	Richard Wright.
6	University of Washington.	18	General Motors.
		19	Romantic (poetry).
7	*Dallas*.	20	*Unforgiven*.
8	A Moor.		
9	Four.		
10	The heart.		

TOTAL

Round Seventy-Five

1 Of which Motown girl group was Diana Ross originally a member?

2 Which British naturalist was the author of *The Origin of the Species*?

3 During the American Revolution, more inhabitants of the American colonies fought for which, the British or the Continental Army?

4 During which President's administration were both Robert Kennedy and Martin Luther King assassinated?

5 In nature eagles and owls are both part of what family?

6 Elvis Presley's mansion, Graceland, is located in which U.S. city?

7 From which U.S. state did former Vice-President and Presidential candidate Dan Quayle hail?

8 Hamburger University is run by what U.S. corporation?

9 What was the name of the Ancient Greek goddess of love and beauty?

10 Which television series featured the characters Maddie Hayes and David Addison?

11 Who was the Commander of the ill-fate Apollo 13 mission to the Moon?

12 In rock music, how many band members were in the group Ben Folds Five?

13 A dodecagon is a shape with how many sides?

14 In sports, how many former USFL teams transferred to the NFL when the league folded?

15 What is the name of the residence of the Mayor of New York City?

16 A quintet is formed of how many musicians?

17 In Geography, in which African country would you find the Kruger National Park?

18 CBC is the state-owned television network of which country?

19 In anatomy, how many teeth does a typical adult human have?

20 In 1999 the oil giant Exxon merged with what other oil company?

PREVIOUS TOTAL

125,000

75,000

50,000

25,000

10,000

5,000

2,500

1,000

BANKED

TOTAL

Answers

1	The Supremes.	11	James (Jim) Lovell.
2	Charles Darwin.	12	Three.
3	British.	13	Twelve.
4	Lyndon (Baines) Johnson.	14	Zero.
5	Raptors (Birds of Prey).	15	Gracie Mansion.
6	Memphis (Tennessee).	16	Five.
7	Indiana.	17	South Africa.
8	McDonalds.	18	Canada.
9	Aphrodite.	19	32.
10	*Moonlighting*.	20	Mobil.

Round Seventy-Six

1 In federal politics, how many justices sit on the Supreme Court?

2 In musical instruments, how many valves does a trumpet traditionally have?

3 The Erie Canal links Lake Erie with which New York river?

4 In history, who founded the Free French movement in 1940 and went on to become the first President of France's Fifth Republic?

5 Which actress played the character of Sally Bowles in the 1971 film *Cabaret*?

6 In ancient Athens the death penalty was put upon anyone cutting down what type of tree?

7 In what year was the first Woodstock music festival held?

8 In which country would you find the Inca ruins of Macchu Picchu?

9 In baseball, the designated hitter plays in which of the major leagues: American League or National League?

10 In the Orson Welles' film *Citizen Kane*, who or what was Rosebud?

11 In Literature, who was the the author of the 1925 novel *The Great Gatsby*?

12 In anatomy, is the coccyx located near to the spine or near to the feet?

13 What mathematical theorem describes the square of the hypoteneuse as equal to the sum of the squares of the other two sides?

14 In politics, what does does the acronym OAS stand for?

15 Which NFL team became known as "America's Team" in the 1960s?

16 In entertainment, Emilio Estevez is the son of which *West Wing* actor?

17 Lee Iacocca was the CEO of what automobile manufacturer during the 1980s?

18 What "C" is a squirrel like rodent native to the mountains of South America?

19 How many quarts are there in the US measure of one gallon?

20 The Berkley School of Music is located in what US city?

Answers

1	Five.	12	The spine.
2	Three.	13	The Pythagorean (Pythagoras') theorem.
3	Hudson (River).		
4	Charles de Gaulle.	14	Organization of American States.
5	Liza Minnelli.		
6	Olive (tree).	15	Dallas Cowboys.
7	1969.		
8	Peru.	16	Martin Sheen
9	American League.	17	Chrysler.
10	A sled.	18	Chinchilla.
11	F(rancis). Scott Fitzgerald.	19	Four.
		20	Boston (Mass).

PREVIOUS TOTAL

125,000

75,000

50,000

25,000

10,000

5,000

2,500

1,000

BANKED

TOTAL

Round Seventy-Seven

1 In sports, what record-breaking footballer's nickname was "Sweetness"?

2 The author Joseph Conrad wrote which book that was later turned into the Francis Ford Coppola movie *Apocalypse Now*?

3 In U.S. politics, the elephant is the symbol of which political party?

4 In *The Wizard of Oz*, what did the Lion want to ask the Wizard for?

5 In what European city is rock legend Jim Morrison's grave located?

6 In what state would you find Clemson University's main campus?

7 In music, how many sharps and flats are there in a C Major scale?

8 Kabuki Theatre originated in what country?

9 In what year did Neil Armstrong become the first person to step on to the moon?

10 In anatomy, where is your uvula located: in the stomach or in the throat?

11 Jewish holidays begin at which time of day: sunrise or sunset?

12 In music, Keith Moon was the drummer for which British rock band?

13 In what U.S. city was the sport of basketball founded in?

14 Which Old Testament character had a coat of many colours?

15 In what police series did the actor Johnny Depp once appear regularly?

WEAKEST LINK

16 TV sports announcer John Madden coached which NFL team to win the Super Bowl?

17 In business, Juan Trippe was the founder of what now-defunct airline?

18 In higher education, what does the acronym M.I.T. stand for?

19 At over 4,000 miles long, what is the world's longest river?

20 What 1970s folk singer and 1990s religious and political activist had hits with "Moonshadow" and "Wild World?"

PREVIOUS TOTAL

125,000

75,000

50,000

25,000

10,000

5,000

2,500

1,000

BANKED

TOTAL

Answers

1 Walter Payton.

2 *Heart of Darkness*.

3 Republican Party.

4 Courage.

5 Paris.

6 South Carolina.

7 None.

8 Japan.

9 1969.

10 The throat.

11 Sunset.

12 The Who.

13 Springfield (Mass).

14 Joseph (son of Jacob).

15 *21 Jump Street*.

16 Oakland Raiders.

17 Pan Am (Pan American Airways).

18 Massachusetts Institute of Technology.

19 (River) Nile.

20 Cat Stevens (Yusuf Islam).

Round Seventy-Eight

1   In TV, Michael J. Fox starred as Alex P. Keaton in what 1980s sitcom?

2   Bobby Knight spent most of his career coaching basketball at which school?

3   In higher education, what does the qualification "Ph.D." stand for?

4   In geography, Juneau is the capital of which U.S. state?

5   For which movie comedy did Marisa Tomei win an Oscar for Best Supporting Actress?

6   The broadcaster NHK is a public television network in which country?

7   On July 7, 1939, the U.S. Lighthouse Service merged with what other Federal organization?

8   Kurt Cobain was the lead singer of what Seattle-based grunge band?

9   Playwright Arthur Miller was married to which blonde actress in the 1950s?

10 In football, quarterback Joe Montana played his professional career with the San Francisco 49ers and which other team?

11 In science, a single unit of energy or work is called what?

12 Other than gold and frankincense what was the other gift presented by the Three Wise men to baby Jesus in Bethlehem?

13 Pol Pot was the leader of which Cambodian political group during the 1970s?

14 Which television detectives were played by Sharon Gless and Tyne Daly?

15 In business, the U.S. broadcaster NBC is owned by what manufacturing conglomerate?

16 The House of Windsor are the reigning monarchs what European country?

17 AU is the chemical symbol for what precious metal?

18 The comedy troupe "Second City" originated in which city?

19 The airline Asiana is based in what country?

20 Which Shakespeare play opens with the line "When shall we three meet again, in thunder, lightning or in rain?"

125,000

75,000

50,000

25,000

10,000

5,000

2,500

1,000

BANKED

Answers

1	*Family Ties.*	11	A joule.
2	University of Indiana.	12	Myrrh.
		13	Khmer Rouge.
3	Doctor of Philosophy.	14	Cagney and Lacey.
4	Alaska.	15	General Electric.
5	*My Cousin Vinny.*		
6	Japan.	16	United Kingdom (Great Britain).
7	U.S. Coast Guard.	17	Gold.
8	Nirvana.	18	Chicago.
9	Marilyn Monroe.	19	Korea.
10	Kansas City Chiefs.	20	*Macbeth.*

TOTAL

Round Seventy-Nine

1 In sports, who was the last Major League baseball pitcher to win 30 games in a single season?

2 McGill University is an English-speaking University in what French-speaking city?

3 In history, Paul Revere's famous ride took place during which US war?

4 In politics, what does the acronym GOP stand for?

5 In music, the tune *Take Five* was written by what jazz musician?

6 Which mountain is the highest in the European Alps?

7 The ulna and radius are two bones located in which part of the body?

8 During World War II what was the name of the "unbreakable" code machine used by the Axis powers that became the subject of a movie in 2001?

9 *The Age of Innocence* and *The House of Mirth* are novels by which American author?

10 The rock singer Alannis Morissette comes from which country?

11 In AD 79 the Roman city of Pompeii was destroyed by the eruption of what volcano?

12 The "Longhorns" the nickname of what southern university's sport teams?

13 In politics, Senator Jesse Helms represented which eastern state?

14 Created by the novelist Anne Rice the Vampire Lestat was played by which actor in the film *Interview with the Vampire*?

15 In medicine, the study of the bumps on a person's head is know as what?

16 Showman William Frederick Cody was better known by which name?

17 In track and field, how many events are there in the heptathlon?

18 In geography, Patagonia is a region located in which South American nation?

19 The MCAT is an examination generally taken before attending what type of graduate school?

20 What singer released an album in the 1970s called *Songs in the Key of Life*?

PREVIOUS TOTAL

125,000

75,000

50,000

25,000

10,000

5,000

2,500

1,000

BANKED

TOTAL

Answers

1	Denny McLain.	12	University of Texas.
2	Montreal.		
3	Revolutionary War.	13	North Carolina
4	Grand Old Party.	14	Tom Cruise.
		15	Phrenology.
5	Dave Brubeck.	16	Buffalo Bill.
6	Mont Blanc.	17	Seven.
7	The arm.	18	Argentina.
8	Engima.	19	Medical school.
9	Edith Wharton.	20	Stevie Wonder.
10	Canada.		
11	(Mount) Vesuvius.		

Round Eighty

1   In TV, what *Square Pegs* actress went on to star in *Sex in the City*?

2   President Lyndon Baines Johnson hailed from what US state?

3   *The Colbys* was a spin-off of which successful television drama series?

4   The first five books of the Old Testament are known as what to followers of Judaism?

5   In music, how many members are there in the band Rush?

6   What "A", a semi-precious stone, was long believed to prevent baldness?

7   Prior to JFK, who was the last U.S President to be assassinated?

8   In literature, what American novel surrounds the relationship between a southern boy and a slave named Jim?

9   In geography, Puget Sound is located in which U.S. state?

10 The Dayton Accord refers to a 2000 peace treaty for the conflict in which European country?

11 In 1066, which battle was fought between the English and the Norman invaders headed by William the Conqueror?

12 The comedy movie *Caddyshack* has what sport as its central theme?

13 In music, what country singer and "Man in Black", had a big hit with his song "I Walk the Line?"

14 In higher eduction, Rutgers is the state university of which state?

15 What "D" is the triangular alluvial deposit at the mouth of a river?

16 In television, what was the name of Fred Flintstone's daughter on *The Flintstones*?

17 In sports, who was the baseball player with the nickname of the "Splendid Splinter?"

18 In demographics, what is the most populous country in Africa?

19 The Soviet government boycotted which 1980s summer Olympic Games as a tit-for-tat reaction to the US boycott of the previous games?

20 Legendary soccer player Pele appeared for which North American Soccer League team in the 1970s?

Answers

1	Sarah Jessica Parker.	11	(Battle of) Hastings.
2	Texas.	12	Golf.
3	*Dynasty*.	13	Johnny Cash.
4	The Torah (five books of Moses).	14	New Jersey.
5	Three.	15	Delta.
6	Amethyst.	16	Pebbles.
7	William McKinley.	17	Ted Williams.
8	*Huckleberry Finn*.	18	Nigeria.
9	Washington.	19	1984 (Los Angeles).
10	Kosovo.	20	New York Cosmos.

PREVIOUS TOTAL

125,000

75,000

50,000

25,000

10,000

5,000

2,500

1,000

BANKED

TOTAL

Round Eighty-One

1 In geography, in what state is at the easternmost point of the U.S.?

2 In politics, the Central African Republic was most recently a colony of what European nation?

3 The style of music known as "bossa nova" originated in which country?

4 Where in West Virginia was abolitionist John Brown was ambushed in 1859?

5 In astronomy, the Sea of Tranquility is located on what celestial body?

6 The TV series *St. Elsewhere* was set in a hospital in what city?

7 In literature, what author wrote the novel *Franny and Zooey*?

8 In geography, the city of Baku lies on what interior sea?

9 Who won the Oscar for Best Actor for his portrayal of the King in the musical *The King and I*?

10 In the animal kingdom, what bug shares its name with a sport that includes bowling and wickets?

11 Which American swimmer won seven gold medals at the 1972 Olympics?

12 What city has the largest subway system in the world?

13 What has been the most common surname for India's Prime Ministers since the country gained independence?

14 From which country does the rock band U2 originally come from?

15 What incident caused the deaths of rock 'n' roll stars Buddy Holly, The Big Bopper and Ritchie Valens?

16 In theater, what was the longest running show on Broadway?

17 The "Head of the Charles" is a race in which collegiate sport?

18 What is the last word of the Pledge of Allegiance?

19 The Heisman Trophy is awarded annually to the best player in which collegiate sport?

20 Name the World War II general who was known as "Old Blood and Guts"?

PREVIOUS TOTAL

125,000

75,000

50,000

25,000

10,000

5,000

2,500

1,000

BANKED

TOTAL

Answers

1	Maine.	14	Ireland.
2	France.	15	An airplane crash.
3	Brazil.	16	*Cats.*
4	Harper's Ferry.	17	Crew (rowing).
5	The Moon.	18	All.
6	Boston.	19	Football.
7	J.D.Salinger.	20	General (George) Patton.
8	Caspian Sea.		
9	Yul Brynner.		
10	The cricket.		
11	Mark Spitz.		
12	Moscow.		
13	Gandhi.		

Head-to-Head

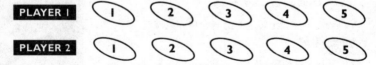

Player I

1 In 1994, the comet Shoemaker-Levy Nine crashed into what planet?
2 In television, what was the name of Fred's boss on *The Flintstones*?
3 Which tall Cy Young-award winning Baseball Pitcher is known as "The Big Unit?"
4 Cincinnati International Airport is actually located in which U.S. State?
5 Which writer has had several novels published under the pen-name of Richard Bachman?

Player 2

1 In chemistry, what is the lightest and most abundant element in the Universe?
2 The first woman to be featured on a federally-minted U.S. coin was which Spanish queen?
3 What wine used in making Martinis is derived from the German word meaning "woodworm?"
4 In 1976, Idi Amin allowed hijackers of a French airliner to land at which airport in Uganda?
5 The name of what U.S. State comes last alphabetically?

Answers	
Player I	**Player 2**
1 Jupiter.	1 Hydrogen.
2 Mr. Slate.	2 Isabella (Isabella I).
3 Randy Johnson.	3 Vermouth.
4 Kentucky.	4 Entebbe (International).
5 Stephen King.	5 Wyoming.

Head-to-Head

PLAYER 1

PLAYER 2

Player 1

1 The Nintendo character known as Mario first appeared in which arcade video game?

2 What literary detective first appeared in the 1887 novel *A Study in Scarlet*?

3 What is the name of the protective metal glove used in the Middle Ages that was said to be "thrown down" as a sign of a challenge?

4 What Supreme Court Chief Justice administered the Presidential Oath to George W. Bush?

5 In movies, who directed *A Clockwork Orange*?

Player 2

1 Vladimir Nabokov's novel *Lolita* was originally written in what language?

2 Known for its blue box, which company manufactures the NFL's Super Bowl trophy?

3 Actor Danny Thomas founded a children's hospital named after what patron saint of hopeless causes?

4 In algebra, what diagrams, named after a British mathematician, use overlapping circles to show the relationship between sets?

5 In ten-pin bowling, a total of how many consecutive strikes make up a perfect game?

Answers	
Player 1	**Player 2**
1 Donkey Kong.	1 English.
2 Sherlock Holmes.	2 Tiffany (& Co).
3 Gauntlet.	3 St. Jude.
4 William Rehnquist.	4 Venn (Boolean) diagrams.
5 Stanley Kubrick.	5 Twelve.

Head-to-Head

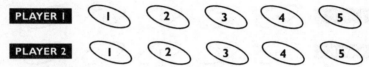

PLAYER 1 1 2 3 4 5

PLAYER 2 1 2 3 4 5

Player 1

1   In politics, which U.S. state has the most electoral votes?

2   What is the name of the RCA mascot dog that appears in the painting "His Master's Voice?"

3   Which ancient Greek philosopher was forced to drink hemlock in 399 B.C.?

4   The tulip flower gets its name from a Turkish word for what traditional Muslim headdress?

5   Which TV sitcom took place at a fictional Nantucket airline called Sandpiper Air?

Player 2

1   What woman became the Philippines' president in 1986 after Ferdinand Marcos fled the country?

2   Which breed of domestic canine has a name that is German for "badger dog?"

3   In television, who created the show *Star Trek*?

4   In Japan, the clothing items known as *getas* are worn on which part of the body?

5   In music, which vocalist had a hit with the single "Don't Worry, Be Happy"?

Answers	
Player 1	**Player 2**
1 California.	1 Corazon Aquino.
2 Nipper.	2 Dachshund.
3 Socrates.	3 Gene Roddenberry.
4 Turban.	4 The foot (feet).
5 *Wings*.	5 Bobby McFerrin.

Head-to-Head

PLAYER 1

PLAYER 2

Player 1

1 What is the only U.S. State name that ends with three vowels?

2 In music, what Latin percussionist titled his 100th album *The Mambo King*?

3 In sports, an Olympiad is defined as a span of how many years?

4 In television, which male actor replaced Michael J. Fox on *Spin City*?

5 In literature, what Russian-born scientist wrote the *Foundation Trilogy*?

Player 2

1 Which American city is nicknamed "The Big Easy?"

2 What English legal term means to take away an attorney's right to practice law due to unethical conduct?

3 In the U.S. Army, what do the letters in the acronym AWOL stand for?

4 In the movie *A Cry in the Dark*, the character played by Meryl Streep claims that her baby was taken by which type of Australian wild dog?

5 What movie rental chain is listed on the New York Stock Exchange under the symbol B.B.I.?

Answers	
Player 1	**Player 2**
1 Hawaii.	1 New Orleans.
2 Tito Puente.	2 Disbar (Disbarment).
3 Four.	3 Absent Without Leave.
4 Charlie Sheen.	4 Dingo.
5 Isaac Asimov.	5 Blockbuster

Head-to-Head

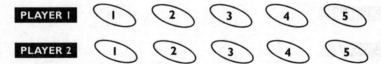

PLAYER 1 1 2 3 4 5

PLAYER 2 1 2 3 4 5

Player 1

1 In fashion, what U.S. designer is known for her "Lizwear" and "Lizgolf" clothing lines?

2 What fictional town is the setting for the Archie comic books?

3 In science absolute zero is equal to how many degrees Kelvin?

4 In nature, what is the smallest citrus fruit?

5 Who directed the Oscar-winning movie *Crouching Tiger, Hidden Dragon*?

Player 2

1 In movies, Hugh Jackman played which superhero in the film *X-Men*?

2 What fitness program did Judy Sheppard Missett create by blending jazz dance and exercise?

3 In the dice game craps, Boxcars refers to rolling two of what number?

4 In mythology, Cupid was the Roman counterpart to which winged Greek God of Love?

5 What judicial body of military personnel are convened to try members of the U.S. armed forces?

Answers	
Player 1	**Player 2**
1 Liz Claiborne.	1 Wolverine (Logan).
2 Riverdale.	2 Jazzercise.
3 Zero.	3 Six.
4 Kumquat (Cumquat).	4 Eros.
5 Ang Lee.	5 Court martial.

Head-to-Head

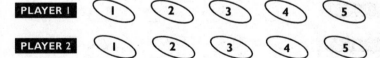

PLAYER 1   1   2   3   4   5

PLAYER 2   1   2   3   4   5

Player 1

1   In math, what is 1⅓ × 3?

2   In movies, what actor played the title character in both *Beetlejuice*?

3   What rock band featured original members Paul Stanley, Peter Criss, Gene Simmons and Ace Freely?

4   Which French town is home to the shrine where the Virgin Mary is said to have visited St. Bernadette?

5   In 1519, what Portuguese explorer led the first successful circumnavigation of the Earth?

Player 2

1   Which Japanese Prime Minister approved the attack on Pearl Harbor?

2   In television, what resident of the Planet Melmac became part of the Tanner family?

3   Which actress starred as an evil nanny in *The Hand That Rocks the Cradle*?

4   What brand of car, named for the French founder of Detroit, redesigned its wreath and crest logo in 2001?

5   Which rock group recorded the song "Heart of Glass" with lead singer Debbie Harry?

Answers	
Player 1	**Player 2**
1 Four.	1 (Hideki) Tojo.
2 Michael Keaton.	2 Alf (Alien Life Form).
3 Kiss.	3 Rebecca De Mornay.
4 Lourdes.	4 Cadillac
5 Ferdinand Magellan	5 Blondie

Head-to-Head

PLAYER 1

PLAYER 2

Player 1

1 In business, actress Melanie Griffith is a spokesperson for which cosmetic company founded by Charles Revson?

2 In history, who is credited with introducing pipe-smoking to England?

3 Knute Rockne coached the "Four Horsemen" in the football backfield of what University?

4 In Disney's *Snow White and the Seven Dwarfs*, which dwarf has no beard?

5 The title characters in the play *Rosencrantz and Guildenstern Are Dead* were first minor parts in which work by William Shakespeare?

Player 2

1 The *Adelaide News* and *Sunday Mail* were the first two papers owned by what media titan?

2 Meaning "the Bay of Smoke," what city is the world's northernmost capital?

3 In thoroughbred racing, which legendary jockey won his first Kentucky Derby in 1955 and his last in 1986?

4 Who was the first host of NBC's late-night talk show called *Tomorrow*?

5 Which physicist was Director of the Laboratory at Los Alamos during the development of the first atomic bomb?

Answers	
Player 1	**Player 2**
1 Revlon.	1 Rupert Murdoch.
2 Sir Walter Raleigh.	2 Reykjavik
3 Notre Dame.	3 Willie (Bill) Shoemaker.
4 Dopey.	4 Tom Snyder
5 *Hamlet.*	5 Robert Oppenheimer.

Head-to-Head

| PLAYER 1 | 1 | 2 | 3 | 4 | 5 |
| PLAYER 2 | 1 | 2 | 3 | 4 | 5 |

Player 1

1 What series of children's books features Flossie, Freddy, Nan and Bert?

2 Which snacks are named for the clergyman who invented them to cure lust?

3 The Egyptian Museum in Berlin houses the limestone bust of what ancient Queen of Egypt and mother of two other queens?

4 According to Jerry Falwell's *National Liberty Journal*, which Teletubby was reported to be a Gay role model.

5 What is the only New England state without an Atlantic coastline?

Player 2

1 In geography, which major river touches six countries on its way from the Swiss Alps to the Dutch North Sea coast?

2 What charity group, founded by Reverend Edgar Helms, has more than 1,700 stores nationwide?

3 According to the Latin phrase "in vino veritas", one can find truth in what?

4 In the play *Six Degrees of Separation*, the character Paul pretends to be the son of which African-American actor?

5 In math, a store that stays open 24 hours a day is open how many hours per week?

Answers	
Player 1	**Player 2**
1 *Bobbsey Twins.*	1 The Rhine
2 Graham Crackers.	2 Goodwill (International).
3 Nefertiti.	3 Wine.
4 Tinky Winky.	4 Sidney Poitier
5 Vermont.	5 168.

Head-to-Head

PLAYER 1   1   2   3   4   5

PLAYER 2   1   2   3   4   5

Player 1

1 The name of which brand of toy trucks is the Sioux Indian word for "Great?"

2 In the book of Genesis, Noah's Ark measured 300 x 50 x 30 in which ancient unit of length?

3 In politics, the British Parliament is composed of the Sovereign, the House of Lords and what legislative body?

4 Which poem by Alfred Tennyson includes the line "Into the Valley of Death rode the six hundred?"

5 In sports, who was the first baseball player ever paid $100,000 a season?

Player 2

1 Albert Einstein rejected an offer in 1952 to become president of what Middle East nation?

2 The computer language Fortran was named by combining what two words?

3 In movies, who directed *GoodFellas*?

4 An Act of Congress in 1963 allowed whose portrait to be replaced by John F. Kennedy's on U.S. half dollar coins?

5 What U.S. Commonwealth celebrates its discovery by Christopher Columbus on November 19?

Answers	
Player 1	**Player 2**
1 Tonka.	1 Israel.
2 Cubit.	2 Formula Translator.
3 House of Commons.	3 Martin Scorsese.
4 *Charge of the Light Brigade*.	4 Benjamin Franklin.
5 Joe DiMaggio.	5 Puerto Rico.

Head-to-Head

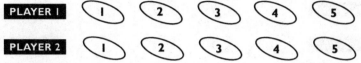

PLAYER 1   1   2   3   4   5

PLAYER 2   1   2   3   4   5

Player 1

1 Which actor who was nominated for the Best Actor Oscar for his role in *The Insider?*

2 In literature, which author won a Pulitzer Prize for *Siddhartha?*

3 Which legendary basketball player turned professional with the name Lew Alcindor?

4 In demographics, which of the United States' bordering countries has the largest population?

5 Which country singer was the subject of the movie *Coal Miner's Daughter?*

Player 2

1 Which country's parliament, the Althing, is the world's oldest, having been established in 930AD?

2 Which star of the *Fresh Prince of Bel Air* TV series had a lead role in the movie *Men in Black?*

3 In music, which grunge band's first album was called *Bleach?*

4 In the 1980s, what Super Bowl-winning football team produced the "Super Bowl Shuffle?"

5 In education, which Ivy League university has its main campus in New York City?

Answers	
Player 1	**Player 2**
1 Russell Crowe.	1 Iceland.
2 Hermann Hesse.	2 Will Smith
3 Kareem Abdul-Jabbar.	3 Nirvana.
4 Mexico.	4 Chicago Bears.
5 Loretta Lynn.	5 Columbia University.

Head-to-Head

| PLAYER 1 | 1 | 2 | 3 | 4 | 5 |
| PLAYER 2 | 1 | 2 | 3 | 4 | 5 |

Player 1

1   In the animal kingdom, a vixen is a female of which type of mammal?

2   In geography, where would you find the counties of Mayo and Donegal?

3   What U.S. city was the site of rioting protesters, at a World Trade Organization Conference?

4   In music, what is the last name of country singing sisters Louise, Irlene and Barbara?

5   Founded in 1924, what department store's name includes the street of its New York City address?

Player 2

1   What "M" is a bottle-size used for wine or champagne that holds two-fifths of a gallon?

2   In tourism, the Rock and Roll Hall of Fame is located in what city?

3   Who was the U.S. president before John F. Kennedy?

4   In geography, the surface of which sea is the lowest point on Earth?

5   The Tar Heels is the nickname of which university's sports teams?

Answers

Player 1	Player 2
1 Fox.	1 Magnum.
2 (Republic of) Ireland (Eire).	2 Cleveland.
3 Seattle.	3 Dwight D. Eisenhower.
4 Mandrell.	4 The Dead Sea.
5 Saks Fifth Avenue.	5 North Carolina.

Head-to-Head

| PLAYER 1 | 1 | 2 | 3 | 4 | 5 |
| PLAYER 2 | 1 | 2 | 3 | 4 | 5 |

Player 1

1 The motor manufacturer Volvo has its headquarters in what country?

2 What actor won the Best Actor Oscar for his roles in *Philadelphia* and *Forrest Gump*?

3 In business, what does the acronym of AT&T stand for?

4 What author is acknowledged to have written the first mystery starring a fictional detective?

5 In theater, what British town was the birthplace of William Shakespeare?

Player 2

1 In music, what band was was famous for the song "Mister Roboto?"

2 In what city was the battle of Bunker Hill fought?

3 In the animal kingdom, what color is a lobster's blood?

4 In demographics, what country is the most populous democracy?

5 In film, which Canadian comedy actor died during the filming of *Wagons East?*

Answers

Player 1	Player 2
1 Sweden.	1 Styx.
2 Tom Hanks.	2 Boston.
3 American Telephone and Telegraph.	3 Blue.
4 Edgar Allan Poe.	4 India.
5 Stratford-Upon-Avon.	5 John Candy.

Head-to-Head

PLAYER 1

PLAYER 2

Player 1

1 In baseball, which player holds the Major League record for the most career hits?

2 In television, the medical drama series *E.R.* is set in what American city?

3 In music what group's only top 10 single was "Touch of Grey?"

4 In the military, what is the highest award offered by the British armed forces?

5 In movies, what was the name of Dorothy's dog in *The Wizard of Oz*?

Player 2

1 In music, from what country did the rock band INXS originate?

2 What John Hughes movie involves characters attending a Saturday morning detention?

3 The University of Michigan's main campus is located in which city?

4 In sports, what championship-winning NBA team played in Minneapolis until 1960?

5 In television, what does the acronym BBC stand for?

Answers

Player 1		**Player 2**	
1	Pete Rose.	1	Australia.
2	Chicago.	2	*The Breakfast Club.*
3	The Grateful Dead.	3	Ann Arbor.
4	The Victoria Cross.	4	(Los Angeles) Lakers.
5	Toto.	5	British Broadcasting Corporation.

Head-to-Head

| PLAYER 1 | 1 | 2 | 3 | 4 | 5 |
| PLAYER 2 | 1 | 2 | 3 | 4 | 5 |

Player 1

1   What is the main currency of Italy?

2   The star sign Libra is represented by which symbol?

3   In music what is the name of Tina Turner's former husband and singing partner?

4   What mail delivery group lasted only from April 1860 to October 1861 and was considered a complete failure?

5   In the animal kingdom, what mammal gives birth to the largest baby?

Player 2

1   In movies, what legendary artifact is Indiana Jones searching for in the film *Indiana Jones and the Last Crusade*?

2   What is the capital of Saskatchewan province?

3   In politics, to what nation did Alaska formerly belong?

4   In professional boxing, how long is each round in a championship contest?

5   In television, where would you find Oscar the Grouch?

Answers

Player 1	Player 2
1 Lira.	1 The Holy Grail.
2 Scales.	2 Regina.
3 Ike.	3 Russia (Soviet Union).
4 The Pony Express	4 Three minutes.
5 Blue whale.	5 Sesame Street.

Head-to-Head

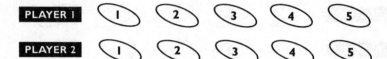

| PLAYER 1 | 1 | 2 | 3 | 4 | 5 |

| PLAYER 2 | 1 | 2 | 3 | 4 | 5 |

Player 1

1 In television, what was Bill Cosby's profession in *The Cosby Show* which ran in the 1980s?

2 In sports, what NBA team won the most championships in the 1990s?

3 In movies, what was the title of Spike Lee's first film as a director?

4 In geography, which two oceans are linked by the Panama Canal?

5 What US city is credited with inventing the psychedelic sound?

Player 2

1 In movies, what was the first name of Humphrey Bogart's character in *Casablanca*?

2 What country singer started Farm Aid to benefit U.S. farmers?

3 What document, essential to the future of the U.S., was signed on September 17, 1787?

4 What former Buffalo Bills quarterback became the Secretary of Housing and Urban Development?

5 What two journalists from the *Washington Post* newspaper wrote *All The President's Men*?

Answers	
Player 1	**Player 2**
1 Obstetrician.	1 Rick.
2 Chicago Bulls.	2 Willie Nelson
3 *She's Gotta Have It*.	3 The Constitution.
4 Atlantic and Pacific (Oceans).	4 Jack Kemp.
5 San Francisco.	5 (Carl) Bernstein and (Bob) Woodward

Head-to-Head

PLAYER I

PLAYER 2

Player I

1 In history, what U.S. city was initially named, Fort Dearborn, Indian Territory?

2 In music, what multi-persona funk singer had the hit album *Purple Rain*?

3 In literature, what was the first American novel to sell one million copies?

4 In politics, what was the first country to give women the vote in 1893?

5 In baseball, who holds the record for most games played consecutively? Cal Ripken (Jr.).

Player 2

1 What was the first "talkie" movie?

2 In music, which British band originally recorded the hit "My Generation"?

3 In geography, where would you find Wilkes Land?

4 In politics, which political leader runs the Rainbow Coalition party?

5 Who, in 1980, shot to death the former Beatle John Lennon?

Answers	
Player I	**Player 2**
1 Chicago.	1 *The Jazz Singer.*
2 Prince.	2 The Who.
3 *Uncle Tom's Cabin.*	3 Antarctica.
4 New Zealand.	4 Rev. Jesse Jackson.
5 Cal Ripken (Jr.).	5 Mark (David) Chapman.

WEAKEST LINK

Head-to-Head

Player 1

1 What was the original name of the legendary boxer Muhammad Ali?

2 Who was the director of the 1987 movie *Wall Street* starring Michael Douglas?

3 Who is the author of the series of books featuring young wizard Harry Potter?

4 In music, which artist has the nickname of the "Godfather of Soul?"

5 In history, which U.S. President created the Tennessee Valley Authority?

Player 2

1 Which Democrat Presidential candidate lost to Ronald Reagan in 1984?

2 Jimmy, Wayne and Marie are all members of which singing family?

3 In television, who hosted the long-running game show *$25,000 Pyramid*?

4 In physics, what is lighter a proton or an electron?

5 Which American author won the Nobel Prize for Literature in 1962?

Answers	
Player 1	**Player 2**
1 Cassius (Marcellus) Clay.	1 John F. Kennedy.
2 Oliver Stone.	2 The Osmonds.
3 J.K. (Joanne) Rowling.	3 Dick Clark.
4 James Brown.	4 Electron.
5 Franklin D. Roosevelt.	5 John Steinbeck.

Head-to-Head

PLAYER 1

PLAYER 2

Player 1

1 In what city was the television series *One Day at a Time* set?

2 In sports, which college basketball team featured the starting lineup known as the "Fab Five?"

3 Who was the arch-enemy of Sir Arthur Conan Doyle's sleuth Sherlock Holmes?

4 In movies, which actor and dancer was the star of *An American in Paris* and *Singin' in the Rain*?

5 In politics, which president created the interstate highway system?

Player 2

1 Which U.S. state was the first to give the vote to African-Americans?

2 In which novel by Charles Dickens would you find the characters of Fagin and the Artful Dodger?

3 Which rock 'n' roll band originally recorded "Rock Around the Clock?"

4 In sports, what baseball team has won the most World Series?

5 In movies, who directed the 1997 multi-Oscar winning hit *Titanic*?

Answers	
Player 1	**Player 2**
1 Indianapolis.	1 Iowa.
2 University of Michigan.	2 *Oliver Twist*.
3 Professor Moriarty.	3 Bill Haley And The Comets.
4 Gene Kelly.	4 New York Yankees.
5 Dwight D. Eisenhower.	5 James Cameron

Head-to-Head

| PLAYER 1 | 1 | 2 | 3 | 4 | 5 |
| PLAYER 2 | 1 | 2 | 3 | 4 | 5 |

Player 1

1 Which actor, the son of Donald Sutherland, appeared in *A Few Good Men*?

2 Apiphobia is the fear of which insects?

3 Cartman, Kenny, Stan and Kyle are characters in which animated television series?

4 Which President created the U.S. Parks system?

5 Who is the lead singer of the group Pearl Jam?

Player 2

1 In politics, who ran as the Republican opponent of Bill Clinton in the 1996 Presidential election?

2 In movies, who was the director of the 1994 film *Pulp Fiction*?

3 Who was the tenor saxophonist on Miles Davis' *Kind of Blue*?

4 Which NFL (football) of the 1970s had defensive line nicknamed the "Purple People Eaters?"

5 In television, who played Wonder Woman in the 1970s series?

Answers	
Player 1	**Player 2**
1 Kiefer Sutherland.	1 Bob Dole
2 Bees.	2 Quentin Tarantino
3 *South Park*.	3 John Coltrane.
4 Teddy (Theodore) Roosevelt.	4 The Minnesota Vikings.
5 Eddie Vedder.	5 Lynda Carter.

Head-to-Head

Player 1

1 In theater, who was the original phantom in the 1980s broadway musical *Phantom of the Opera*?

2 When Israel achieved independence in 1948, who was the first man to be elected as Prime Minister?

3 In football, who was the first African-American quarterback to win a Super Bowl?

4 Which U.S. President was known as "Old Hickory"?

5 In television news, who was the only American network anchor at the collapse of the Berlin Wall in 1989?

Player 2

1 In boxing, what country hosted "The Rumble in the Jungle?"

2 In theater, who wrote the play *Troilus and Cressida*?

3 In politics, who was Richard Nixon's first Vice President?

4 In movies, who played Holly Golightly in the film *Breakfast at Tiffanys*?

5 In the animal kingdom, "tiger", "reef" and "hammerhead" are types of what?

Answers	
Player 1	**Player 2**
1 Michael Crawford.	1 Zaire.
2 David Ben Gurion.	2 William Shakespeare.
3 Doug Williams.	3 Spiro Agnew.
4 Andrew Jackson.	4 Audrey Hepburn.
5 Tom Brokaw.	5 Shark.

And Finally...

Who, sadly, is out of their depth?

Who, alas, is not burdened with intelligence?

Who has continued to be dazed and confused?

Who has drawn the intellectual short straw?

Which one of your teammates is gumming up the works?

Whose knowledge is very small indeed?

Who's past their best?

Is there a village that needs its idiot back?

Who is least likely to assist you in raising the bank?

Whose education has been a very sorry waste of time?

Who is a nuisance to the rest of the team?

Let me remind you, she who hesitates must be heaved off, he who dithers should be ditched.

Who is allergic to intelligence?

Whose intellectual services are no longer required?

Who's on the road to nowhere?

Who fell off the tree of knowledge?

Who is buckling under the pressure?

I urge you, eject the idiot.